Philosophical Writing

SECOND EDITION

*For my mother and in memory of
my father*

Philosophical Writing
An Introduction

SECOND EDITION

A. P. Martinich
University of Texas at Austin

First edition copyright © Prentice-Hall Inc, 1989
Second edition copyright © A. P. Martinich, 1996

The right of A. P. Martinich to be identified as author of this work has been
asserted in accordance with the Copyright, Designs and Patents Act 1988.

First published 1996

Reprinted 1997 (twice), 1998

Blackwell Publishers Inc
350 Main Street
Malden, Massachusetts 02148, USA

Blackwell Publishers Ltd
108 Cowley Road
Oxford OX4 1JF, UK

Library of Congress Cataloging in Publication Data
Martinich, Aloysius
Philosophical writing: an introduction/A. P. Martinich – 2nd ed.
p. cm.
Includes index.
ISBN 0–631–20281–1 (pbk: alk. paper)
1. Philosophy—Authorship. I. Title.
B52.7.M37 1996 96–7632
808'.0661—dc20 CIP

British Library Cataloguing in Publication Data
A CIP catalogue record for this book is available from the British Library

Typeset in 10.5 on 12.5pt Palatino
by Graphicraft Typesetters Limited, Hong Kong
Printed and bound in Great Britain
by MPG Books Ltd, Bodmin, Cornwall

This book is printed on acid-free paper

Contents

Note to the Second Edition

Writing to a friend, Voltaire apologized for the length of his letter: "If I had had more time, this letter would have been shorter." In revising the sections that appeared in the first edition of this book, I often found ways to make them shorter, and, I think, better. But I also had ideas about how I could add other topics to the book in order to make it better. Primarily these are sections on definition, contraries and contradictories, distinctions, and a glossary of terms that may be helpful in your philosophical writing.

In preparing the second edition, I have happily acquired debts to some of my current and former students who commented on the text: Stephen Brown, Sarah Cunningham, Nathan Jennings, and Lisa Maddry. My wife Leslie, as usual, read the entire manuscript. Also I want to thank my very helpful editor Steve Smith.

Finally, a large part of my thinking and reading about philosophy has been done in Miami Subs and Grill on the Drag. I want to thank the owners, Michael and Lisa Mermelstein, for their hospitality.

Introduction

Philosophical essays may have many different structures. For people accustomed to writing them, the choice of a structure is often neither difficult nor even conscious. The essay seems to write itself. For people unaccustomed to writing them, the choice is often tortured or seemingly impossible. I offer this book to the latter group of people, typically students. And rather than survey many possible structures, I have concentrated on what I think is the simplest, most straightforward structure that a philosophical essay might have. My purpose is to help students write something valuable so that they might begin to develop their own styles. The project is analogous to teaching art students to draw the human hand. The first goal is accuracy, not elegance.

Elegance in writing is not learned. It is the product of a kind of genius, and genius begins where rules leave off. I plan to discuss something that I think is learnable: how to write clear, concise and precise philosophical prose. Elegance is desirable, but so is simplicity. And that is what I aim at.

A philosopher once said, "Half of good philosophy is good grammar." This remark is witty and profound, and, like any good aphorism, difficult to explain. Before I try to explain at least part of what it means, let me forestall a possible misunderstanding. Although good philosophical writing is grammatical, there is virtually nothing about grammar in this book in the sense in which your fifth grade teacher, Mrs Grundy, discussed it. Virtually all students know the rules of grammar, and yet these rules are often flagrantly violated in their philosophical prose. Why does this happen?

One reason is that philosophy often involves the attempt to assign things to their proper categories, and the categories are not clear or are at least difficult to understand. Philosophers have sometimes divided reality into the things that are mental and the things that are material. Sometimes they have divided reality into things that are substances (things that exist on their own) and things that are accidents (things that are properties or depend upon other things for their existence). There is even a grammatical correlation between these categories. Nouns correlate with substances (*man* with man), and adjectives correlate with accidents (*rectangular* with rectangular). When philosophers argue that things that seem to belong to one category really belong to another, grammar is strained. Some philosophers have been shy of saying *God is just* on the grounds that the phrase *is just* expresses a property of God, and God, because of his simplicity, cannot have properties. Yet, because they want to associate justice with God in some way, they have transformed the adjective "just" into the noun *the just* and argue that it is strictly correct to identify God with justice itself and thus to say, "God is the just."

Sometimes the attempt to say something new and correct about the limits of reality causes the grammar to break down completely, as when Martin Heidegger says, "Nothing nothings." The pronoun *nothing* cannot be a verb, so the vocable *nothings* is unintelligible. Further, Heidegger seems to be construing *nothing* as a noun in its first occurrence in the sentence, as if "nothing" named something. (Of course, Heidegger would disagree with my grammatical remarks; and that is just one more reason why philosophy is difficult: it is hard to get philosophers to agree even about grammar.)

Thomas Hobbes was the first to discuss the propensity of philosophers to commit category mistakes by combining words belonging to one category with words belonging to another. To put it roughly, a category mistake is the logical equivalent of mixing apples and oranges. The sentence "Colorless green ideas sleep furiously" involves several category mistakes.

Colorless things cannot be green or any other color; ideas cannot sleep or be awake; and nothing can sleep furiously. These categories just don't mesh. One of Hobbes's examples of a category mistake is "Quiddity is a being." Perhaps we can agree with him that such a sentence is absurd without following out his reasons for this view. Consider another of his examples: "The intellect understands." According to him, *the intellect* is the name of an *accident* or property of bodies, which is one category, while *understands*, even though it is grammatically a verb, is the name of a *body* (humans), which is another category. And thus he holds that the sentence "The intellect understands" is literally absurd. What Hobbes thinks is literally true is the sentence "Man understands by his intelligence."

It is quite possible for someone to disagree with Hobbes about whether the sentence "The intellect understands" makes sense or not, and to criticize Hobbes's philosophico-grammatical view, which underlies his grammatical judgment. Philosophers often disagree about what is absurd and what is not. Consider the sentence "Beliefs are brain states." Does this sentence express a category mistake or a brilliant insight into the nature of the mental? Philosophers disagree. So it is not always easy to say whether some philosophical thesis constitutes a great philosophical insight or a cheap grammatical blunder. Thus, added to the inherent difficulty of philosophy is the difficulty of philosophical writing, which often groans under the burden placed on syntax and semantics.

Students often write patently ungrammatical sentences because that is the way philosophy sounds to them. And it sounds that way because the thought being expressed is radically unfamiliar. There is no comfortable place for that thought in the student's system of beliefs. So the student either situates the thought inappropriately or isolates it from her other, more familiar beliefs. In a word, the thought is strange. As a consequence, when students come to explain, criticize, or even endorse that thought, they may be tempted to use incoherent and ungrammatical language, because they have distorted and mutilated the half-understood thought. Their writing, though muddled, is an accurate representation of their understanding.

If you find yourself writing a sentence or paragraph that is grammatically out of control, then your thought is probably out of control. Consequently, you can use your own prose as a measure of the degree to which you understand the issue you are writing about and as an index to the parts of your essay that need more consideration. (I owe the ideas in this paragraph to Charles Young.)

This explanation of why half of good philosophy is good grammar inspires a criterion: good philosophical writing is grammatical. If a person can write a series of consistently grammatical sentences about some philosophical subject, then that person probably has a coherent idea of what he is discussing.

Another related criterion of good philosophical writing is precision. Contrary to the conventional wisdom prevalent among students, vague and verbose language is not a sign of profundity and astuteness but of confusion. Teachers of philosophy who are dedicated to the above criteria in effect issue a challenge to students: write grammatically, clearly, and precisely. Since language is the expression of thought, clear language is the expression of clear thought. Writing style should facilitate the comprehension of philosophy. Style should enhance clarity.

If half of good philosophy is good grammar, then the other half is good thinking. Good thinking takes many forms. The form that we will concentrate on is often called *analysis*. The word *analysis* has many meanings in philosophy, one of which is a method of reasoning (discussed in Chapter 5). Another meaning refers to a method or school of philosophy that reigned largely unchallenged for most of this century. Many people now think that this method is *passé* and that we are now in a postanalytic era. I am not taking a stand on that issue in this book. I use *analysis* in a very broad sense that includes both analytic and postanalytic philosophy. As I use the term, the goal of analytic philosophy is the truth, presented in a clear, orderly, well-structured way. I take a strong stand for clarity, order, and structure. The goal of analysis, in its broad sense, is to make philosophy less difficult than it otherwise would be. This is just a corollary of a more general principle: anyone can make a subject difficult; it takes an accomplished thinker to make a subject simple.

Philosophical writing has taken many forms, including dialogue (Plato, Berkeley, Hume), drama (Camus, Marcel, Sartre), poetry (Lucretius), and fiction (Camus, George Eliot, Sartre). I will discuss only the essay form. There are three reasons for this decision. First, it is the form in which you are most likely to be asked to write. Second, it is the easiest form to write in. Third, it is currently the standard form for professional philosophers. Although the dialogue form is attractive to many students, it is an extremely difficult one to execute well. It tempts one to cuteness, needless metaphor, and imprecision.

It is often advisable to preview a book. That advice holds here. Skim the entire book before reading it more carefully. Depending on one's philosophical background, some parts will be more informative than others. Chapter 1 discusses the concepts of author and audience as they apply to a student's philosophical prose. Both students and their professors are in an artificial literary situation. Unlike typical authors, students know less about their subject than their audience, although they are not supposed to let on that they do. Chapter 2 is a crash course on the basic concepts of logic. It contains background information required for understanding subsequent chapters. Those who are familiar with logic will breeze through it while those with no familiarity with it will need to read slowly and carefully. Chapter 3 discusses the structure of a philosophical essay and forms the heart of the book. The well-worn but sound advice that an essay should have a beginning, a middle, and an end applies to philosophical essays too. Chapter 4 deals with a number of matters related to composing drafts of an essay. Various techniques for composing are discussed. Anyone who knows how to outline, take notes, revise, do research, and so on might be able to skip this chapter. Chapter 5 explains several types of arguments used in philosophical reasoning, such as dilemmas, counterexamples and *reductio ad absurdum* arguments. Chapter 6 discusses some basic requirements that the content of an essay must satisfy. Chapter 7 discusses goals for the form of your writing: coherence, clarity, conciseness and rigor. Chapter 8 discusses some standard problems students have with the first few pages of an essay.

Like essays, most books have conclusions that either summarize or tie together the main strands of the work. It would have been artificial to do so in this case, however, since the book as a whole does not develop one main argument but consists of a number of different topics that should be helpful to the student. However, Appendix A, "It's Sunday Night and I Have an Essay Due Monday Morning," which is supplied for those who bought this book but never got around to reading much of it, could also serve as a conclusion. Many of my students who read the first edition let me know that this was the first part of the book they read, some Sunday night about six weeks into the semester.

In order to serve the needs of a wide range of students, the level of difficulty varies from elementary to moderately advanced. Even within individual chapters, the level of difficulty can vary significantly, although each section begins with the simplest material and progresses to the most difficult. Thus, a chapter on a new topic might revert from complex material in the previous chapter to a simple level. I believe that intelligent, hardworking students can move rather quickly from philosophical innocence to moderate sophistication.

At various points, I have presented fragments of essays to illustrate a stylistic point. The topics of these essay fragments are sometimes controversial and the argumentation provocative. These passages are meant to keep the reader's interest and do not always represent my view. It would be a mistake to focus on the content of these essay fragments when it is their style that is important. Also, it is quite likely that the reader will disagree with a few or even many of the stylistic claims I make. If this leads readers to at least think about why they disagree, and to discover what they prefer and why, then a large part of my goal will have been achieved.

In the following pages, I often contrast rhetorical elements with logical elements. Going back as far as Socrates, rhetoric has often had a bad name in philosophy. No negative attitude towards rhetoric is implied in this book. "Rhetoric," as I use it, refers to style, that is, to those elements of writing that facilitate communication; and it is a presupposition of this book that these elements are extremely important. After all, like any essay, a philosophical essay that fails to communicate fails in one of its central purposes.

Philosophical Writing is intended to be practical. It is supposed to help you write better and thereby improve your ability to present your thoughts. Since almost any class may require you to write an essay that analyzes some kind of concept, the skills gained in learning to write about philosophical concepts may prove useful in writing other types of essays.

For generic pronouns, I use the following conventions. Male gender pronouns will be used for references to a professor. Female gender pronouns will be used for references to the student.

1

Author and Audience

It might seem obvious who the author and audience of a student's essay are. The student is the author and the professor is the audience. Of course that is true. But a student is not a normal author, and a student's professor is not a normal audience. I want to expand on these two points in this chapter. I will begin with the conceptually simpler topic: the abnormality of a teacher as audience.

1 The Professor as Audience

It's indispensable for an author to know who the audience is. Depending upon the audience, an author might take one or another tack in explaining her position.

A student is not in the typical position of an author for many reasons. While an author usually chooses her intended audience, the student's audience is imposed on her. (The student's predicament, however, is not unique. An audience usually chooses his author. In contrast, the professor's author is imposed on him: his students. Both should make the best of necessity.) Unless the student is exceptional, she is not writing to inform or convince her audience of the truth of the position she expostulates. So her purpose is not persuasion. Further, unless the topic is exceptional or the professor relatively ignorant, the student's purpose is not straightforwardly expositive or explanatory either. Presumably, the professor already understands the material that the student is struggling to present clearly and correctly. Nonetheless, the student cannot presuppose that the professor is knowledgeable about the topic being discussed because the professor, in his role as judge, cannot assume that the student is knowledgeable. It is the student's job to show her professor that she understands what the professor already knows. A student may find this not merely paradoxical but perverse. But this is the existential situation into which the student as author is thrown.

The structure and style of a student's essay should be the same as an essay of straightforward exposition and explanation. As mentioned above, the student's goal is to show the professor that she knows some philosophical doctrine by giving an accurate rendering of it; further, the student must show that she knows, not simply what propositions have been espoused by certain philosophers, but why they hold them. That is, the student must show that she knows the structure of the arguments used to prove a philosophical position, the meaning of the technical terms used and the evidence for the premises. (One difference between the history of philosophy and the history of ideas is that the former cares about the structure and cogency of the arguments.) The student needs to assume (for the sake of adopting an appropriate authorial stance) that the audience is (a) intelligent but (b) uninformed. The student must state her thesis and then explain what she means. She must prove her thesis or at least provide good evidence for it.

All technical terms have to be explained as if the audience knew little or no philosophy. This means that the student ought to explain them by using ordinary words in their ordinary senses. If the meaning of a technical term is not introduced or explained by using ordinary words in their ordinary meanings, then there is no way for the audience to know what the author means. For example, consider this essay fragment:

> The purpose of this essay is to prove that human beings never perceive material objects but rather semi-ideators, by which I mean the interface of the phenomenal object and its conceptual content.

This passage should sound profound for no more than a nano-second. In theory, there is nothing objectionable to introducing the term *semi-ideator*, but anyone with the gall to invent such a neologism owes the reader a better explanation of its meaning than "the interface of the phenomenal object and its conceptual content." In addition to neologisms, words with ordinary meanings often have technical meanings in philosophy, e.g.

determined
matter
ego
universal
reflection
pragmatic

When an author uses a word with an ordinary meaning in an unfamiliar technical sense, the word is rendered ambiguous, and the audience will be misled or confused if that technical meaning is not noted and explained in terms intelligible to the audience.

It is no good to protest that your professor should permit you to use technical terms without explanation on the grounds that the professor knows or ought to know their meaning. To repeat, it is not the professor's knowledge that is at issue, but the student's. It is her responsibility to show the professor that she knows the meaning of those terms. Do not think that the professor will think that you think that the professor does not understand a term if you define it. If you use a technical term, then it is your term and you are responsible for defining it. Further, a technical term is successfully introduced only if the explanation does not depend on the assumption that the audience already knows the meaning of the technical term! For that is precisely what the student has to show.

There is an exception. For advanced courses, the professor may allow the student to assume that the audience knows what a beginning student might know about philosophy, perhaps some logic or parts of Plato's *Republic* or Descartes's

Meditations, or something similar. For graduate students, the professor may allow the student to assume a bit more logic, and quite a bit of the history of philosophy. It would be nice if the professor were to articulate exactly what a student is entitled to assume and what not, but he may forget to do this, and, even if he remembers, it is virtually impossible to specify all and only what may be assumed. There is just too much human knowledge and ignorance and not enough time to articulate it all. If you are in doubt about what you may assume, you should ask. Your professor will probably be happy to tell you. If he is not, then the fault lies with him; and you can rest content with the knowledge that, in asking, you did the right thing. That is the least that acting on principle gives us; and sometimes, alack, the most.

While I have talked about who your audience is and about how much or how little you should attribute to him, I have not said anything about what attitude you should take toward the audience. The attitude is respect. If you are writing for someone, then you should consider that person worthy of the truth; and if that person is worthy of the truth, then you should try to make that truth as intelligible and accessible to him as possible. Further, if you write for an audience, you are putting demands on that person's time. You are expecting him to spend time and to expend effort to understand what you have written; if you have done a slipshod job, then you have wasted his time and treated him unfairly. A trivial or sloppy essay is an insult to the audience in addition to reflecting badly on you. If a professor is disgruntled when he returns a set of essays, it may well be because he feels slighted. A good essay is a sign of the author's respect for the audience.

2   The Student as Author

Although you are the author of your essay, you must not be intrusive. This does not mean that you cannot refer to yourself in the first person. Whether you do or not is a matter of taste. Some decades ago, students were forbidden to use "I" in an essay. A phrase like "I will argue" was supposed to be replaced with a phrase like "My argument will be" (or "The argument of this paper" or "It will be argued"). Formal writing is more informal these days. "My argument will be" is verbose and stilted. I prefer "I will argue" for an additional reason. Although physical courage is widely admired and discussed in contemporary society, and, perhaps, unwittingly caricatured in macho men, intellectual courage is not. Too few people have the courage of their convictions; yet convictions on important issues that are the result of investigation and reflection deserve the courage needed to defend them.

Ideas have consequences just as surely as physical actions do. Some are good, some are bad; some are wonderful, some are horrid. Own up to yours.

A person who writes, "It will be argued," is passive; he is exhibiting intellectual courage obliquely at best. By whom will it be argued? If it is you, say so. A person who writes, "I will argue," is active. She is committing herself to a line of reasoning and openly submitting that reasoning to rational scrutiny.

Philosophical writing is virtually never autobiography, even when it contains autobiographical elements (*The Confessions* of St Augustine and those of Jean-Jacques Rousseau are notable but rare exceptions). It is very unlikely then that your personal life or personal feelings should be exposed in your philosophical writing, at least in those terms. No philosopher should care how you *feel* about the existence of God, freedom, abortion or anything else, presented merely as your feelings. Thus, use of the phrase, *I feel*, is with rare exception forbidden in essays. Your feelings have no claim to universality and do not automatically transfer to your audience. You might feel that God exists but that is no reason why anyone else should. The phrase, *I argue*, in contrast, does transfer. The phrase implies that the author has objective rather than merely subjective grounds for her position and thus that the audience ought to argue in the very same way.

Specific incidents in your life also have no place in your essay, considered as *your* experiences. Considered simply as *experiences,* they may have both relevance and force. Contrast these two ways of making the same point:

> When I was 14 I wanted a ten-speed bike but needed $125 to buy one. The only way I could get the money legally was to work for it. I hired myself out at $2.00 an hour doing various jobs I hated, like cutting lawns, washing windows and even baby-sitting. It took three weeks, but I finally had enough money to buy the bicycle. What I discovered, often as I was sweating during my labors, was that money is not just paper or metal; it is control over other human beings. The people who hired me were controlling my life. I figured out something else: if I have money and also respect someone, I shouldn't force him to do crummy jobs just so they can get my money.

> Suppose a young person wants to buy something, say, a ten-speed bicycle. He may hire out his services for money, perhaps at $2.00 an hour cutting lawns, washing windows or baby-sitting. By hiring himself out, he is putting himself within the control of the person who is paying him. Money, then, is not simply metal or paper; it is a means of controlling the behavior of other human beings. Further, if a person respects others, he will avoid hiring people for demeaning and alienating labor.

Although the first passage is livelier and more appropriate in nonphilosophical contexts, for example, a newspaper or magazine article, its philosophical point is made more obliquely than in the second, where the author's view of money is directly related to every human being and not just the author. Thus, the second passage is preferable for an explicitly philosophical essay. The first passage is egocentric; the persona of the author is the student herself. In the second passage, the persona of the author is an objective observer of the human condition.

The notion of a persona is a technical one. The word *persona* comes from the Latin word for the mask that actors wore on stage. There were masks for comic and tragic characters, for gods and mortals. To have a persona is to play a role. An author plays a role and hence has a persona. The question is, What is that persona? or What should that persona be? because there are two possible roles an author can have in her essay.

An author inescapably has the role of creator since she is responsible for the words of her essay. As the creator, the author has a transcendent perspective on her essay. In addition, the author has the possibility of being a character in her own essay, not as she appears when she says, "I will argue," but as a character in the examples and scenarios she constructs in order to illustrate or prove a point. Such characters in scenarios have an immanent perspective, and if the author is a character in one of them, then her perspective is immanent also. The status of an author *vis-à-vis* the scenarios she invents is completely different from the status she has as a character in them. I urge you not to abandon your status of inventor.

To change the figure of speech, the author of an essay acts like God. All the characters in the examples are like creatures. When God said, "Let there be light," there was light; and when God said, "Let the earth produce every kind of living creature," there was every kind of living creature. Similarly, when an author says, "Suppose Smith and Jones have their brains interchanged," Smith and Jones have their brains interchanged. God's will cannot be thwarted; whatever God wants to happen happens. He cannot make a mistake; He cannot be deceived. It would be incoherent to write:

> God said, "Let there be light," but He was not quite sure that there was light; He thought there was light but He might have been mistaken.

Like God, an author's will in constructing an example cannot be thwarted if what she says is coherent and if she has no doubts about what she is supposing. The transcendent position of an author is inherently anti-skeptical. A story is told about an eighth grader who was having trouble learning algebra. The teacher said, "Suppose that x equals 2." The student became quite anxious because she thought the teacher could have been wrong or at least overlooking a possibility: "Teacher, suppose that x does not equal 2." The student did not realize that when a person supposes something to be true for the sake of argument, then it is true within the context of that discussion. For all intents and purposes, an author is omnipotent and omniscient (I am speaking only of philosophical authors; some contemporary fiction tries to undermine the seemingly divine qualities of authors). However, omnipotence is limited by logical coherence. Be on guard against thinking that you have proven a point by constructing a logically contradictory scenario, as in this essay fragment:

> Suppose that there is a four-sided plane figure, all the angles of which are square. Further suppose that each point of its perimeter is equidistant from a point inside of it. Thus it follows that there is a round square.

This scenario is defective because its supposition is contradictory. An omnipotent God cannot make a stone too heavy for Him to lift; and this is no limitation of his power.

Continuing the theological analogy, we can say that the characters in a philosophical example, like creatures, are subject to error and deception. ("Suppose that Smith, who has known Jones for 20 years, sees someone who looks exactly like Jones walking across the plaza. Further suppose that Smith does not see Jones, but Jones's long-lost twin brother, although Jones himself is also walking across the plaza out of Smith's sight. . . .") The characters in philosophical examples are the puppets of the authorial gods.

If an author makes herself a character in one of her examples, then she takes on two roles; she confusingly assumes diametrically opposed personas, that of author and that of character (or creator and creature). Consider the following passage:

Suppose that Smith and I have our brains interchanged. And I think that I am Smith and he thinks that he is I. However, I think I remain myself because I am identical with my body at any given time.

It is very difficult to understand this passage, because the reference of "I" shifts between the author *as a character in the scenario* to the author *as the creator of the scenario*. Contrast the original with this revision in which references to the author as a character are replaced with references to a purely created character:

Suppose that Smith and Jones have their brains interchanged. And Jones believes that he is Smith and Smith believes that he is Jones. Nonetheless, I argue that Jones remains Jones and Smith remains Smith, because a person is identical with his body at any given time.

Even this passage can be improved. There is something tendentious about saying "Jones remains Jones and Smith remains Smith" that was not obvious in the first passage. The following third version is better:

Suppose that Smith and Jones have their brains interchanged. And the body that Jones had before the brain interchange believes that it is Smith, and the body of Smith that it is Jones. Nonetheless, I argue that the body of Jones remains Jones and Smith's body remains Smith because a person is identical with his body at any given time.

The point is that the more objective the author's standpoint the better (recall that I am speaking about the above passages rhetorically and am not passing judgment on their cogency). There is never any need for an author to cast herself in her own examples: Smith and Jones, and White, Black, Brown and Green are versatile philosophical character actors. (It is a

substantive issue whether the duality of personas has philosophical consequences; see Thomas Nagel, *The View from
Nowhere*, New York: Oxford University Press, 1985.)

In this chapter, I have tried to explain the sense in which a
student's audience, the professor, must be considered ignorant; and the sense in which the student, a philosophical author,
should maintain a transcendent perspective, from which she
is omniscient and omnipotent. How is that for a Hegelian
reversal?

2

Logic and Argument for Writing

In his *Poetics*, Aristotle remarks that a well-constructed dramatic plot must reflect an action which is "whole and complete in itself and of some magnitude." He goes on to define a whole as "that which has a beginning, middle, and end." Though Greek tragedy and philosophical prose may seem like quite disparate fields of literary endeavor, Aristotle's advice applies to writing a philosophical essay.

Just as the core of a dramatic work is its plot, the core of a philosophical essay is its argument. And just as a good play will have a well-demarcated beginning, middle, and end, so too will a good essay. The beginning of a philosophical essay introduces the argument; the middle elaborates it; the end summarizes it. But what is an argument?

Every competent speaker of English has some idea of what an argument is. And most, upon reflection, would realize that *argument* is in fact equivocal; that is, it has more than one sense. In one sense, it is roughly synonymous with *quarrel* and in another sense roughly synonymous with *reasoning*. In theory, philosophers engage only in the latter, although in practice they sometimes stumble into the former.

The philosophically relevant sense of *argument* has been made more precise by logicians, who, in the course of 2,500 years, have discovered quite a bit about arguments. Although this is not a logic text, a little logic is crucial for understanding the structure of a philosophical essay. (For a brief, but fuller account than given here, I recommend the second edition of Wesley Salmon's *Logic*, Englewood Cliffs, NJ, Prentice-Hall, 1981; for a full account I recommend *Logic and Philosophy* by Howard Kahane, Belmont, CA: Wadsworth, 1984.)

1 What is a Good Argument?

At the simplest level, there are two kinds of arguments: good ones and bad ones. A good argument is one that does what it is supposed to do. A bad argument is one that does not. A good argument is one that shows a person a rational way to go from true premises to a true conclusion, as well as the subject allows (some subjects more easily or certainly show the way than others, say, mathematics more than aesthetics). As explained here, a good argument is relative to a person. What might legitimately lead one person to a conclusion might not lead another person to the same conclusion because so much depends upon the person's background beliefs. What a contemporary philosopher or physicist would recognize as a good argument is often not what an ancient Greek, even Plato, Aristotle, Ptolemy, or Euclid would recognize. Also, there may be good arguments that the ancient Greeks could recognize as good arguments that we could not. For obvious reasons I can't think of an example.

The notion of a "good argument" is an intuitive one. In this chapter I want to make this intuitive notion progressively more precise by considering the following definitions:

Df(1) An argument is a sequence of two or more propositions of which one is designated as the conclusion and all the others of which are premises.

Df(2) A sound argument is an argument which is valid and which contains only true premises.

Df(3) An argument is valid if and only if it is necessary that if all the premises are true, then the conclusion is true.

Df(4)   A cogent argument is a sound argument that is recognized to be such in virtue of the presentation of its structure and content.

Each of these definitions contains key technical terms and ideas that need to be explained, including *proposition* and *valid*. Let's begin by looking at Df(1), the definition of *argument*. Notice that an argument is characterized as a sequence of propositions. Although *proposition* could be given a more technical formulation, for our purposes it is enough for us to understand this term as equivalent to "a sentence that has a truth-value;" that is, it is a sentence that is either true or false. Propositions are sometimes contrasted with questions and commands, which cannot be true or false. *Proposition* is often used interchangeably with *statement* and *assertion* even though the meanings of these words can be different in important ways.

Returning to the definition of *argument*, we should notice that an argument is a *sequence* of propositions because the propositions are supposed to be related in some logically significant way. One of these propositions will be designated as the conclusion; that is, the proposition that is to be proven. Within the context of an essay as a whole, the conclusion is the thesis. Since subordinate propositions within the essay may have to be proved, these subordinate propositions may also be conclusions with their own sets of supporting premises. The premises are the propositions that lead to the conclusion. They provide the justification for the conclusion.

The above definition is abstract. Let's make it a bit less so by considering an extremely spare argument:

All humans are mortals.
Socrates is a human.
_____

Therefore, Socrates is mortal.

The first two sentences are premises. The third is the conclusion, as indicated by the word *therefore*. The premises are supposed to provide the rational force for accepting the conclusion. While this is a good argument, it is rhetorically lame. No one would seriously argue for such an obvious conclusion. It rarely happens that three simple sentences constitute a rationally persuasive argument, which typically requires elaboration and embellishment. Yet, at the beginning of our study, it is wise to keep the matter as simple as possible.

The definition of *argument* in Df(1) is neutral with respect to the issue of whether an argument is defective (bad) or not. Some arguments are defective and some are not. Our goal is to understand the nature of all arguments by concentrating on what constitutes a good one. We then understand what a defective argument is by identifying how it fails to measure up to the criteria for good arguments. As Parmenides said, "The ways of falsehood are infinite, while the way of truth is one."

To further refine the definition of a good argument, let's now consider the concept of a sound argument given in Df(2):

> **Df(2) A sound argument is an argument which is valid and which contains only true premises.**

As this definition makes clear, there are two aspects to a sound argument: validity and truth. An argument is unsound in either of two cases: if it is invalid or if one or more of its premises are false. Thus, to show that your argument is sound, you must show that the argument is valid and show that the premises are true. Since a sound argument is partially defined in terms of the technical notion of validity, we need a definition of it:

> **Df(3) An argument is valid if and only if it is necessary that if all the premises are true, then the conclusion is true.**

To put this in a slightly more colloquial form, the conclusion of a valid argument must be true whenever all its premises are true. The truth of the premises guarantees the truth of the conclusion.

In Df(3), validity is defined in terms of truth and necessity. Further, in Df(4) a cogent argument is partially defined in terms of a sound argument; and a sound argument is partially defined in Df(2) in terms of an argument; and an argument is partially defined in Df(1) as consisting of premises and a conclusion. This process of defining one thing in terms of other things cannot go on forever, no more than the stability of the earth can be explained by saying that it sits on the back of an elephant that rests on the back of another elephant, that rests on the back of another elephant, *ad infinitum*. At some point, the process of explanation must end. (Under all the elephants is a tortoise; and that is the end of it).

As regards validity (and hence soundness and cogency), the process of explanation ends with truth and necessity. These two concepts are being taken as basic and will not be defined. I am relying upon our common understanding of the notions of truth and necessity to carry us. This is not to say that these notions are not problematic; it is just that one must stop somewhere. Cogency, soundness, and validity could have been defined using some other terms and then some terms other than truth and necessity would have been basic and undefined.

There is nothing objectionable in leaving some terms undefined. Indeed, it is inescapable. In order to *say* anything, one must assume that the meanings of *some* words are understood. (This may form the foundation for a paradox involving how it is possible for people to learn a language if one must already know words before one can say anything; fortunately, such a possible paradox is not our problem here.) In every enterprise, one eventually gets to a point at which something must be accepted without definition or argument. If the arguer and arguee cannot agree on any such point, there is a sense in which an argument cannot get started. However, although neither *truth* nor *necessity* will be defined, a little more can and will be said about validity in section 2 of this chapter.

A sound argument is a valid argument with true premises. Yet, many sound arguments are unhelpful because they are not recognizable as good arguments. To incorporate the aspect of recognizability into our intuitive notion of a good argument, we must introduce the idea of a *cogent* argument, as spelled out in Df(4):

Df(4) **A cogent argument is a sound argument that is recognized to be such in virtue of the presentation of its structure and content.**

There are many reasons why a rational person might not recognize a good argument. If its logical form is too complex for any human being to recognize or the evidence needed to show that the premises are true is simply not available, a sound argument would necessarily fail to be cogent, because the condition of recognizability would be impossible to satisfy. However, many sound arguments are, as a matter of fact, not cogent because they are not properly formulated and/or adequate evidence is not adduced in support of key premises. Proper formulation of an argument involves its structure: the argument must be valid and the premises and conclusion must be set out in such a way that its validity is apparent. The matter of evidence, on the other hand, is related to an argument's content and involves once again the notion of truth. Each individual premise must be true and the evidence presented must make this clear.

The intuitive notion of a good argument that we started with at the beginning of this chapter has now evolved into the notion of a cogent argument. We can now summarize by saying that a good (i.e. cogent) argument involves three things: formal validity (structure), true premises (content), and recognizability. This is what you should strive for in your writing. If any one of these elements is missing, your argument will not be cogent. All of these elements are individually necessary and jointly sufficient to produce a cogent argument. In section 3 of this chapter we will examine the notion of cogency in more detail. For now we need to return to a fuller treatment of the crucial notion of validity, the aspect of an argument related to its structure or form.

2   Valid Arguments

Recall the definition of a valid argument given in section 1:

Df(3)   An argument is valid if and only if it is necessary that if all the premises are true, then the conclusion is true.

To repeat what was said earlier, in a valid argument true premises guarantee a true conclusion. A valid argument *cannot* have true premises and a false conclusion. Validity preserves truth. The situation is different when one or more of the premises is false. In such cases, the conclusion might be true or false. In other words, there are valid arguments that have

(a)   true premises and true conclusion;
(b)   false premises and false conclusion;
(c)   false premises and true conclusion.

Let's look at an instance of each of these possibilities (for the sake of illustration, exercise whatever tolerance necessary to assume that the premises in the following examples are true or false as indicated).

Example of a valid argument
with true premises and a true conclusion

Justice is fairness.
Fairness is distributing rewards according to merit and
    penalties according to blame.

Justice is distributing rewards according to merit and
    penalties according to blame.

Example of a valid argument
with false premises and a false conclusion

Justice is what the strong desire.
What the strong desire is what is good for the strong.

Justice is what is good for the strong.

Example of a valid argument
with false premises and a true conclusion

Justice is what the strong desire.
What the strong desire is distributing rewards
  according to merit and penalties according to blame.

Justice is distributing rewards according to merit and
  penalties according to blame.

In each of these examples of a valid argument, the conclusion is related to the premises in a fairly straightforward way. This need not be the case.

Although it is counterintuitive, there are valid arguments in which the premises and conclusion are not related in any plausible way. There are two types of valid arguments in which the conclusion is wholly unrelated to the premises. One type occurs when the conclusion is a *tautology*, that is, a trivially true proposition; that is, a true proposition that is by its nature uninformative. Consider the statement, "Either Aristotle is a great philosopher or he is not." Since this proposition is trivially true, there can be no argument with true premises and it as a false conclusion, no matter how irrelevant the premises are to that conclusion. For example, the argument

Ima Hogg was a great philanthropist.

Either Aristotle is a great philosopher or he is not.

is valid, even though the premise has no apparent topical or evidential relation to the conclusion. This argument is defective and hence not cogent. Yet, it is a valid argument.

The other type of valid argument with topically unrelated

premises and conclusion is one which contains contradictory premises. (Roughly, a proposition is contradictory when it asserts and denies the same thing, e.g. "Aristotle is a great philosopher and he is not a great philosopher.") For example, consider this argument:

Aristotle is a great philosopher and he is not
a great philosopher.

No philosopher has ever made a mistake.

This argument is valid because it satisfies the definition of validity even though the conclusion is unrelated to the premise. When an argument contains a contradictory premise, then that premise is necessarily false, and hence it is not possible for all the premises to be true and the conclusion false. More generally, even if there is no single contradictory premise, so long as the premises are jointly contradictory, the argument is valid.

The fact that every argument with contradictory premises is valid shows that the actual truth of the premises and the argument's validity are separate issues and should not be confused. However, don't be dismayed that every argument with contradictory premises is valid. Every argument with contradictory premises is also unsound since not all the premises can be true together. At least one of the premises must be false.

To say that an argument is valid is to say that the premises *entail* the conclusion. But upon what does entailment depend? One answer is that entailment depends upon the meanings of the words making up the propositions of the argument. Two types of words might be distinguished: topic neutral and topic specific.

Topic specific words include those that are typically first thought of as words, such as *dog, cat, walks, yellow, happily,* as well as more emotionally charged words such as *disarmament, deficit, abortion,* and *fraternity*. What all these words have in common is that they specify or restrict some topic. A sentence with the word *dog* in it, for example, in some very general sense, might be said to have a dog or dogs as one of its topics.

The logic that is concerned with the entailment properties of topic specific words might be called material logic. Thus, material logic is concerned with the entailment that holds between

This object is yellow

and

This object is colored.

Topic specific words that are very general or central to our conceptual scheme, e.g. *goodness, truth, justice, beauty, person, object,* are the traditional topics of philosophy, and the study of their contribution to the entailments of propositions is largely what philosophy is about. Thus, a philosopher might worry about the nature of knowledge by asking whether

x knows that *p*

entails

x believes that *p*.

And he might worry about the nature of truth by asking whether

"S" is true

entails

"S" corresponds to some fact.

When philosophers formulate questions or pose problems in terms of whether one thing entails another, they may be involved in a very traditional philosophical pursuit.

Let's now consider some topic neutral words. *Not, and, or, if . . . then, if and only if, all,* and *some,* are topic neutral in the sense that they do not restrict the topic or subject matter under discussion. Further, they are not restricted with regard to what topic specific words they can combine with to form sentences. The logic that is concerned with the entailment properties of topic neutral words is called *formal logic*. For example, each of these arguments is valid for the same reason:

If John is rich, then Mary is happy.
John is rich.

Mary is happy.

If smoking causes lung cancer, then people
    should not smoke.
Smoking causes lung cancer.

People should not smoke.

If humans are aggressive by nature, then a strong
    government is needed to protect humans
    from themselves.
Humans are aggressive by nature.

A strong government is needed to protect humans
    from themselves.

It does not matter that each of these arguments concerns a different topic. Each is valid for the same reason. Given the meaning of *if . . . then*, any argument or pattern of this form is valid:

$$\text{If } p, \text{ then } q$$
$$\frac{p}{q}$$

where "p" and "q" represent propositions.

The form of argument we have been looking at above is one of the most intuitive argument forms there is. It is called *modus ponens*, which loosely translated means *the mode of affirming*. *Modus ponens* is one of a number of inference forms that constitute the core of *natural deduction systems of propositional logic*. Roughly, propositional logic, sometimes called *the propositional calculus,* can be defined as the logic of some uses of *not, and, or, if ... then* and *if and only if.* These words figure crucially in some of the most basic forms of argumentation that people use. Here, they are presented schematically:

Modus ponens	Modus tollens
If p, then q	If p, then q
p	Not q
———————	———————
q	Not p
Disjunctive syllogism	*Hypothetical syllogism*
p or q	If p, then q
Not p	If q, then r
———————	———————
q	If p, then r
Constructive dilemma	*Destructive dilemma*
If p then q; and if r then s	If p then q and if r then s
p or r	Not q or not s
———————	———————
q or s	Not p or not r

Logic typically includes special symbols for the most important topic neutral words. There is no one set of symbols that is used by a majority of logicians. Different logicians use different symbols for the same topic neutral words. Here are some examples:

Propositional Connective	Symbol	Symbol	Symbol
not	~	¬	—
and	&	·	∧
or	v		∨
if ... then	⊃		→
if and only if	≡		↔

If the symbols in the first column are substituted for their English equivalents, then the argument forms just presented look like this:

Modus ponens	*Modus tollens*
p ⊃ q	p ⊃ q
p	~q
———	———
q	~p
Disjunctive syllogism	*Hypothetical syllogism*
p v q	p ⊃ q
~p	q ⊃ r
———	———
q	p ⊃ r
Constructive dilemma	*Destructive dilemma*
(p ⊃ q) & (r ⊃ s)	(p ⊃ q) & (r ⊃ s)
p v r	~q v ~s
———	———
q v s	~p v ~r

Since these forms are of their very nature abstract, it may be helpful to give an example of each of them. Let's begin with *modus ponens*:

If Hobbes is an empiricist, then Hobbes holds that
   sense knowledge is the foundation for all knowledge.
Hobbes is an empiricist.
—————————————————————————————————
Hobbes holds that sense knowledge is the foundation
   for all knowledge.

Let's now consider an instance of *modus tollens*, which bears some similarity to *modus ponens*.

If Hobbes is an empiricist, then Hobbes holds that
sense knowledge is the foundation for all knowledge.
Hobbes does not hold that sense knowledge is the
foundation for all knowledge.

Hobbes is not an empiricist.

Modus ponens and *modus tollens* are clearly related. Often a
philosophical problem can be summarized as a dispute over
whether the sound argument concerning a certain issue should
be formulated as a *modus ponens* or a *modus tollens* argument.
One could imagine a dispute involving the argument examples above. One person might be using the *modus ponens*
argument to prove that Hobbes emphasizes the importance
of observation in science. His opponent might use the *modus
tollens* argument to prove that Hobbes is not an empiricist.
There is a saying in philosophy: One person's *modus ponens* is
another person's *modus tollens*. Obviously much more would
be involved in the debate than merely these two arguments.
Although both arguments are fairly obviously valid, it is not
obvious which, if either, is sound, and hence neither argument is cogent. As a matter of fact, the instance of *modus
tollens* is the sound argument, and could form the core of a
cogent argument if it were buttressed with evidence showing that Hobbes himself emphasized the deductive and *a priori*
aspects of science.

Let's now consider an example of disjunctive syllogism:

Either Hobbes is an empiricist or he is a rationalist.
Hobbes is not an empiricist.

Hobbes is a rationalist.

This argument is of course valid. Is it sound? A frequent
defect of arguments that have the form of disjunctive syllogism is that not all the relevant alternatives are specified in
the disjunctive proposition. If the disjunctive proposition
does not exhaust all the possibilities, then it may well be false.

For example, is every philosopher either an empiricist or a rationalist? Isn't it possible for a philosopher to be neither? A large part of this issue will depend upon how the terms *empiricist* and *rationalist* are defined. So, if our example of a disjunctive syllogism has any hope of forming the core of a cogent argument, it is necessary to define those terms even though this alone would not suffice (see Chapter 5, section 1, "Definitions").

Hypothetical syllogisms are often used to line up series of dependencies, for example,

If every human action is causally determined, then no human action is free.
If no human action is free, then no human is responsible for any of his actions.

If every human action is causally determined, then no human is responsible for any of his actions.

Although the formal rule of a syllogism dictates that there be only two premises, as in the above example, several hypothetical syllogisms can, however, be strung together to yield a result like this:

If every event is causally determined, then every human action is causally determined.
If every human action is causally determined, then no human action is free.
If no human action is free, then no human is responsible for any of his actions.
If no human is responsible for any of his actions, then it makes no literal sense to praise or blame humans for their actions.

If every event is causally determined, then it makes no literal sense to praise or blame humans for their actions.

When propositions are linked in this sort of way and the conclusion is either counterintuitive or otherwise unacceptable, the challenge lies in determining where and how to break the chain.

Let's now consider the two rules of dilemma. Constructive dilemma might be thought of as two instances of *modus ponens* connected:

$$\frac{(p \supset q) \;\&\; (r \supset s)}{p \lor r}$$
$$q \lor s$$

Similarly, destructive dilemma might be thought of as two instances of *modus tollens* disjoined:

$$\frac{(p \supset q) \;\&\; (r \supset s)}{\sim q \lor \sim s}$$
$$\sim p \lor \sim r$$

Let's now consider an example of each, beginning with constructive dilemma:

> If determinism is true, then actions are neutral with
>   respect to praise or blame; and if humans have
>   free will, then science is limited in what it can
>   explain about reality.
> Either determinism is true or humans have free will.
> _____
> Either actions are neutral with respect to praise or
>   blame or science is limited in what it can explain
>   about reality.

Just as one man's *modus ponens* is another man's *modus tollens*, one man's constructive dilemma is another man's destructive dilemma. The above example of constructive dilemma is easily transmuted into an example of destructive dilemma:

If determinism is true, then human actions are neutral
with respect to praise or blame; and if humans have
free will, then science is limited in what it can
explain about reality.
Human actions are not neutral with respect to praise
or blame, or science is not limited in what it can
explain about reality.

Either determinism is not true or humans do not have
free will.

Genuine philosophical examples of dilemmas typically conclude with a disjunction of unpleasant alternatives. That is
what makes the argument a dilemma in the ordinary sense
of the term, in contrast with the logical sense we have been
discussing. Dilemmas will be discussed again in Chapter 5.

Now that we have a better understanding of what constitutes a valid argument form, let's return to the main issue of
this chapter, namely, what makes up a cogent argument.

3 Cogent Arguments

Recall the definition of a cogent argument in section 1:

**(Df4) A cogent argument is a sound argument that is
recognized to be such in virtue of the presentation of its structure and content.**

A cogent argument is one that compels the audience to accept
its conclusion in virtue of his recognition that the argument
is valid and the premises true. Cogent arguments are person
relative. This would come out more clearly if we reformulated
our definition like this:

**An argument is cogent for an audience just in case that
audience recognizes it to be such.**

The same argument might be cogent to one person and not
cogent to another. All cogent arguments are persuasive to

the audience that recognizes them. Yet not all persuasive arguments are cogent. People are often persuaded by bad arguments and fallacious reasoning.

An argument may be sound, and yet fail to be cogent because its soundness is not recognized. An argument might be this way necessarily, either through the complexity of form that outstrips human comprehension or through the impossibility of gathering evidence needed to show that its premises are true. We are not really interested in these non-cogent arguments, since there is nothing humans can do about them. If humans *cannot* recognize the validity, and the evidence is *in no way* available, then that is the end of it. These arguments, however, should not be confused with others.

There are also some sound arguments that are in fact not recognizable as such either because (1) although their logical structures are not recognized, they could be if they were explained, or because (2) although their premises are not recognized as true, they could be if the evidence which is available were provided. About these kinds of unrecognized sound arguments something can be done: the author can explain their logical structures and provide the evidence for their premises.

All of this can be made clearer with an example. There is no doubt that it is easy to provide a sound argument for the proposition "God exists" (if He does exist). And there is no doubt that it is easy to provide a sound argument for the proposition, "God does not exist" (if He does not exist). Thus, one (*but only one*) of the following two arguments is sound.

First Argument

Either God exists or December 25 is Easter.
December 25 is not Easter.
___
God exists.

Second Argument

Either God does not exist or December 25 is Easter.
December 25 is not Easter.
___
God does not exist.

Now it should be obvious that *neither* of these arguments is cogent even though one of them is sound. The problem is that the sound argument, whichever one it is, is not making itself known! Each argument is clearly valid. Both are instances of disjunctive syllogism. And the second premise of each argument is true. The locus of the problem is the first premise. If God exists, then the first premise of the First Argument is true in virtue of that very fact; and then the First Argument is sound. If God does not exist, then the first premise of the Second Argument is true in virtue of that very fact, and then the Second Argument is sound. But which is it?

Unfortunately, there is nothing in either argument that allows us to determine which is sound. There is nothing in either argument that rationally forces us to accept its first premise. Thus, neither argument is cogent. It is the author's duty to forge sound arguments into cogent arguments. Typically, this requires elaboration: either explanation of the argument's validity or evidence for the truth of the premises.

How might an author try to strengthen one of the above arguments? Although I will usually try to give examples of how to do things correctly, in this case, I will explain how things might go wrong. One can also learn from one's mistakes.

Since the same sort of strategies would apply to either argument, let's consider just the first one. What the First Argument needs is evidence that is sufficient to establish that the first premise is true. What kind of evidence would accomplish this goal? The premise is a disjunctive proposition. As such, it is true if either disjunct is true. We already know that the second disjunct is false. Thus, if the premise is true, it must be because its first disjunct is true. But that disjunct "God exists" is identical with the conclusion. Thus, any evidence for the truth of the premise is *eo ipso* evidence for the truth of the conclusion. What this means is that evidence for the premise is superfluous. If one had evidence for the proposition "God exists," then one could apply it immediately to the conclusion without relying on the premises at all.

Suppose someone wanted to defend the cogency of this

argument by claiming that the first premise is true because "God exists" is true and that "God exists" is true because it is self-evident. This defense does not work. It begs the question. That is, the purpose of the argument is to prove that God exists. But the defender wants to assume that very thing to be self-evident.

"Begging the question" is the fallacy of using a proposition both as the conclusion and as either a premise or as expressing evidence for a premise. Here is a blatant example of begging the question:

The National Debt is too large.
_____
The National Debt is too large.

No one is going to be misled by this argument. Most instances of the fallacy of begging the question, like all fallacies, are more subtle. Sometimes the fallacy occurs when the same proposition is expressed in two verbally different ways. For example, to argue

All humans are mortal.
_____
Therefore, all humans will die.

is to beg the question since the premise and the conclusion mean the same.

A more complex and interesting example of begging the question is this:

Whatever the Bible says is true. For the Bible is the Word of God, and the Word of God is true. Further, we know the Word of God is true because the Bible tells us so.

The basic argument is this:

The Bible is the Word of God.
The Word of God is true.
_____
The Bible is true.

The premise, "The Word of God is true," needs to be supported by evidence. But to use "The Bible says so" (that is, "The Bible is true") as expressing that evidence is to beg the question. For, in this context, "The Bible says so" is another way of saying "The Bible is true," which is just what is supposed to be proved. Thus, it cannot be used either as a premise or as evidence for a premise.

What then makes a cogent argument recognizable? I suggest that it involves relevance and informativeness. A cogent argument contains premises that are relevant to the conclusion. Thus, neither of the arguments about the existence of God that were discussed above are cogent because not all their premises were relevant to the conclusion. A cogent argument must also contain premises that are informative. Sometimes premises are informative if they are novel in the sense that the audience was not aware of them until they were seen in the argument. Sometimes premises are informative in a derivative way; they can be informative if the evidence presented for them is novel. Thus, it may not be informative for someone solely to assert, "I exist." Standing alone, it seems trivial. But, when a philosopher like Descartes points out that evidence for this proposition can be found even in the most radically deceptive thoughts that a person can have, then the proposition "I exist" becomes informative in a way it otherwise isn't. It is also informative in its further use in argumentation against skepticism and for the existence of God. Finally, sometimes premises are informative, not because they are individually novel, but because they are organized in a novel way; and the recognition of a novel organization of already known facts can be instructive. In Plato's *Meno*, Socrates gets a slave boy to deduce an astonishing variety of geometrical theorems by beginning with facts the boy already knows. Socrates attributes the boy's surprising knowledge to a reminiscence of knowledge the boy had in an existence prior to his birth. An alternative explanation is that Socrates led the boy to reorganize the knowledge that the boy acquired during his existence on earth, and in reorganizing this knowledge came to know many more things.

Notice that I have not supplied an example of a cogent argument in this section. A trivially cogent argument would not be instructive. And since my audience is diverse, it would be difficult to construct a nontrivial example in less than several pages. I leave the discovery of a cogent argument to each reader, as an exercise.

The upshot of the chapter to this point is that the notion of a sound argument does not fully capture the intuitive notion of a good argument. We need an idea that takes into account that the argument's soundness is recognized, and that is what the idea of a cogent argument does. In the last three sections, several other logical concepts will be explained: consistency and contradiction in section 4, contraries and contradictories in section 5, and the strength of a proposition in section 6.

4 Consistency and Contradiction

Some propositions can be true together or at the same time. For example, the propositions, "George Washington was the first president of the United States" and "Abraham Lincoln was the fourteenth president of the United States," are consistent with each other. Both of them can be true at the same time and in fact they are both true. Consistent propositions may be on the same or a related topic as the sentences about Washington and Lincoln are. But consistent propositions may be on completely unrelated topics, e.g. "George Washington was the first president of the United States" and "A friend of Turgenev gave him the idea for *Fathers and Sons.*" One sentence is about the history of the United States, the other about a Russian literary figure. They are consistent with each other even though they are topically unrelated.

Propositions can be consistent with each other even if one, some, or all of them, are false. The sentence about Turgenev is false but nonetheless consistent with the sentence about Washington, which is true.

Here is a set of sentences that are consistent and all of which are false:

Aristotle discovered America.
Descartes failed his college course in geometry.
Henry Ford signed the Declaration of Independence.
The Cleveland Indians won the 1995 World Series.

As this example shows, consistency is not a guarantee of truth. It is possible for propositions to be consistent with each other, yet not true. Still, it is important for propositions to be consistent. For if propositions are not consistent with each other (that is, if they are *in*consistent), then it is impossible for all of them to be true. And philosophers, and nonphilosophers, should avoid falsity like the plague.

If a set of propositions is inconsistent, then at least one of them is false. Perhaps the easiest sets of inconsistent propositions to identify are those that contain a proposition and its negation:

Turgenev is a novelist.
Turgenev is not a novelist.

It is not necessary to know anything about Turgenev to know that at least one of these propositions is false. The fact that at least one proposition in an inconsistent set must be false is an interesting feature and one that philosophers often exploit. They often try to formulate sets of propositions, each of which seems true, but which are inconsistent. Such sets of propositions are called *paradoxes*.

The Paradox of Freedom and Causality

1   All events are caused.
2   Human actions are events.
3   Some human actions are free, that is, not caused.

The Paradox of Reference and Existence

1   Everything referred to must exist.
2   The name "Hamlet" refers to Hamlet.
3   Hamlet does not exist.

The Paradox of Promising

1 If a person promises to do something, then he has an obligation to do it.
2 If a person has an obligation to do something, then he can do it.
3 Some people sometimes make promises that they cannot keep.

Formulating a philosophical problem as a paradox helps focus the issue. Anyone purporting to solve the problem must say which of the propositions he thinks is false, and why; or he must explain why he thinks that all the propositions are in fact consistent, that is, how it is possible for all of them to be true even though they may not look consistent.

It is not always easy to tell whether propositions that appear to be inconsistent with each other actually are. This is especially true when the seemingly inconsistent propositions are vague, as

British empiricists believed that minds exist.
British empiricists believed that minds do not exist.

It is not clear whether these sentences are inconsistent or not. The reason is that it is not clear whether either sentence is talking about all British empiricists or just some of them. If each sentence is talking about all British empiricists, then the sentences are inconsistent. But if each is talking about some British empiricists, then the sentences express consistent propositions; and in fact would both be true. My own view is that when sentences are vague, it should be said that they do not express a proposition at all; that they express only part of a thought. Since they do not express a complete proposition, they do not have a truth-value and are neither true nor false. This means that they cannot be consistent or inconsistent with each other.

So far I have given examples of consistent and inconsistent sets of propositions that have contained at least two propositions. But these notions also apply to individual propositions. The proposition

Aristotle was a poet

is consistent because it is possible for it to be true, even though it is in fact false. And the proposition

Aristotle was a poet and Aristotle was not a poet

is inconsistent because it is impossible for it to be true. Inconsistent propositions are also called *contradictions*.

Consistency and inconsistency (contradiction) are obviously related ideas. Although it might not be obvious, they are also related to entailment. A proposition *p* entails a proposition *q* just in case *p* is inconsistent with *not q*.

Exercises

1 Choose one of the paradoxes above and explain why the propositions expressed in them are inconsistent.
2 Are the following two propositions consistent or inconsistent with each other?
All British empiricists believe that the mind is a substance.
Some British empiricists believe that the mind is a substance.

5   Contraries and Contradictories

In the last section, contradiction was defined in relation to consistency. A contradiction is a proposition that is inconsistent; and a contradictory set of propositions is a set of propositions that are inconsistent. Contradiction can be defined in other ways, ways that do not mention inconsistency:

A (self-)contradiction is a proposition that cannot be true.
A set of propositions is contradictory just in case there is
no way to make all of them true.

For example, "Socrates is mortal and Socrates is not mortal"
is contradictory; and the set of (two) propositions, "Socrates is
mortal" and "Socrates is not mortal" are contradictory.

For the purpose of contrasting contradictions with contraries, it is convenient to restrict the discussion to pairs of
propositions:

Two propositions are contradictory just in case one must
be true and one must be false.
Two propositions are contrary just in case they cannot
both be true.

These two propositions contradict each other:

The wall is blue.
The wall is not blue.

These two propositions are contraries:

The wall is (completely) blue.
The wall is (completely) red.

Although two contrary propositions cannot both be true, it
is possible for both of them to be false. If the wall is yellow,
then both of the propositions displayed immediately above
are false.

It should be obvious that we can extend the idea of contradictions and contraries to predicates or properties:

Two properties are contradictory just in case one must
be true of an object and one must be false of it.
Two properties are contrary just in case they cannot both
be true of an object.

Being blue/being nonblue are contradictory properties. Being blue/being red are contrary properties.

The distinction between contraries and contradictories is important because they are often mistaken. Although it is unlikely that you will mistake being red and being blue for contradictory properties, you might mistake being rich and being poor as contradictory, or being generous and being stingy. Also it is easy to confuse not being just (a contrary of being just) with being unjust (its contradictory). A cabbage growing in a garden is not just but it is not unjust either.

Some philosophers have used the observation that *being just* and *being unjust* are contraries and not contradictories to help solve the problem of evil. Here is an example of that in an essay fragment:

A Solution to the Problem of Evil

The problem of evil is insoluble until and unless one realizes that justice and injustice are contrary terms and that neither one applies to God. To be just is to be subject to laws and to follow all of those laws that apply. To be unjust is to be subject to laws and not to follow all of those that apply. But God is neither just nor unjust because He is not subject to any law. In order to be subject to law, once must not have control over it. But God has complete control over law since He makes all of the laws and is subject to no constraint with regard to the content of those laws. That is part of what is meant both by the omnipotence and the absolute sovereignty of God. That is why God was not unjust when He told Abraham to kill his son Isaac and not unjust when He allowed Satan to torture Job. Since God can be neither just nor unjust but makes the laws that determine who will be, it is appropriate to say that He is above justice and injustice.

But what else should we say about God with respect to justice and injustice? Since every property has a contradictory and at least one property of each contradictory pair of properties is true of an object, the properties contradictory to being just and being unjust must be true of God. Consequently, God is not just and not unjust.

Let's consider one last pair of terms. Subjectivity and objectivity are often simply assumed to be contradictories. Whether they are contraries or contradictories depends upon how they are defined. One way to guarantee that they are contradictories is to define one of them as not being the other. For example,

> x is subjective if and only if x can be judged by only one
> person and on the basis of her immediate experience.
> x is objective if and only if x is not subjective.

So defined, subjectivity and objectivity are contradictory. But sometimes both are defined independently of each other, such that they turn out to be contraries that are mistaken for contradictories.

> x is subjective if and only if x can be judged by only one
> person and on the basis of her immediate experience.
> x is objective if and only if x is publicly observable.

For example, abstract entities like truth, justice, government, numbers (not to be confused with numerals), and some physical entities like subatomic particles (only the effects of which can be seen) are neither subjective nor objective by the above definitions (see, further, Chapter 5, section 1, "Definitions").

Exercises

1. Given that an atomic sentence is a sentence of which no proper part is a sentence, can an atomic sentence have more than one sentence contradict it? Can an atomic sentence have more than one sentence contrary to it?
2. Categorize the following pairs as contraries, contradictories, or neither:

(a)   tall/short
(b)   tall/nontall
(c)   just/merciful
(d)   just/unjust
(e)   red/tall
(f)   rubber/iron
(g)   merciful/unmerciful
(h)   all powerful/powerful
(i)   happy/unhappy
(j)   responsible/irresponsible
(k)   lawful/unlawful
(l)   male/female
(m)   male/nonmale
(n)   Democrat/Republican
(o)   poor/honest

3   Given the definitions below, are subjectivity/objectivity contraries or contradictories?

x is subjective if and only if there is only one person who can experience x.

x is objective if and only if the properties of x can be determined by more than one person.

6   The Strength of a Proposition

Philosophers often talk about the strength of a proposition. Some propositions are stronger and some are weaker than others. These notions of strength and weakness are technical ones and need to be defined. Although the definitions are not difficult – they require only that you understand the notion of entailment – without these definitions you would be surprised at what philosophers think about the strength or weakness of a proposition.

A proposition p is stronger than a proposition q if and only if p entails q and q does not entail p.

For example, "Most British empiricists believe that the mind is a substance" is stronger than "Some British empiricists believe that the mind is a substance."

A proposition *p* is weaker than a proposition *q* if and only if *p* does not entail *q* and *q* does entail *p*.

Obviously, "Some British empiricists believe that the mind is a substance" is weaker than "Most British empiricists believe that the mind is a substance." Two propositions are equally strong if each entails the other.

There are many propositions that cannot be compared with regard to strength, for example, "Plato was a philosopher" and "David Hume was a philosopher." Neither proposition entails the other. Thus, one is neither stronger nor weaker than the other. Further, although "Every Greek philosopher had an ethical theory" may sound stronger than "It is possible that some philosopher at some time believed some true proposition," in fact it is not, since it does not entail the latter. This does not mean that these two propositions are equally easy or difficult to prove. Indeed, the former would be more difficult to prove, or would at least require much more evidence since it is making a claim about *all* Greek philosophers, while the latter is making a claim about *some* philosopher. Moreover, the evidence for each would be different. If one proposition is stronger than another, then it requires more or better evidence to prove it; but if they cannot be related to each other in terms of strength, then there is no general way of predicting which proposition will require more or better evidence.

It is important for you to know how strong propositions are for several reasons. You need to know how strong each of your premises needs to be in order to prove your case. Premises should not be stronger than you need them to be, because the stronger they are the more evidence they require and typically the more difficult they are to prove. The weaker the proposition, the less evidence one is required to supply. But your premises should also not be too weak, because if they are, then they will not entail your conclusion. Your argument will be invalid. Further, if you try to prove something stronger than is necessary and fail, then either you or your audience may draw the false inference that your position is untenable, even though a weaker set of premises might have been sufficient to entail your conclusion.

Sometimes discovering that something can be proved using a weaker proposition can be a great philosophical discovery. Many philosophers have tried to prove the existence of God by using as a premise, "Something is in motion." John Duns Scotus, in the late-13th century, made a brilliant move when he constructed a proof that uses the weaker proposition "It is possible that something is in motion." This proposition is true so long as the idea of motion does not contain a contradiction. This proposition might be true even if what humans consider motion were an illusion and there were no actual motion in the world. Thus, this proposition has fewer presuppositions than the stronger proposition, "Something is in motion."

Suppose you want to write in favor of skepticism. For our purposes, let's say that it is the view that no human knows anything. Then it is important to decide (know?!) which of the following propositions you need to prove or provide evidence for:

1   Each belief humans have is dubious.
2   Each belief humans have might be dubious.
3   Each belief humans have is false.
4   Each belief humans have might be false.

Proposition 2 is weaker than 1; 4 is weaker than 3. (Is 3 weaker than 2? Is 2 weaker than 4?) A philosopher is in a better initial position if he can get away with proving the weaker of two propositions.

It is also important to know how strong your opponent's proposition is. If your opponent asserts "All British empiricists believe that the mind is a substance," then he is asserting something *quite strong*. This means that his position can be refuted by establishing a relatively weak proposition:

"Some British empiricist does not believe that the mind is a substance." Thus, it would be sufficient for you to show that there is at least one person, for example, David Hume, who is a British empiricist who did not believe that the mind is a substance. On the other hand, if your opponent asserts "Some British empiricists believed that the mind is a substance," then he is asserting something relatively weak, and the truth of the proposition, "Some British empiricist did not believe that the mind is a substance" is *not* sufficient to refute him. Rather, you would have to prove the very strong proposition, "No British empiricists believed that the mind is a substance." I would advise against trying to prove this. In general, the stronger a thesis, the weaker a proposition needs to be to refute it; and the weaker a thesis, the stronger a proposition needs to be to refute it.

Abstractly considered, strong propositions require a lot of evidence, weak propositions require little. In practice, how much evidence is required depends upon the needs of your audience. You must supply as much evidence as your audience needs to be informed and persuaded. Consider this argument for what is a rather strong proposition, namely, that no taxation is justified:

> Nonvoluntary transfers of property are violations of rights. A thief who steals property violates the owner's rights. Taxation is a nonvoluntary transfer of property from the individual to the government. Therefore, the government through taxation is no better than a thief.

Although it is possible that this argument is sound, it would not be cogent for most audiences. For it does not take into consideration any of the relatively obvious arguments against the premise that "taxation is a nonvoluntary transfer of property" (in books on critical reasoning and informal logic, this neglect to mention all the considerations relevant to an issue is called *the fallacy of suppressed evidence*). Consider an essay fragment that is written as a reply to the above passage:

Taxation is not like thievery at all, but rather like a payment for services rendered. People rely upon the government for various services that are essential to the quality of their life, not just police and fire protection, but roads, traffic laws, utilities, civil and criminal courts, and so on. People in business rely on the government even more, e.g. for patent laws and import and export laws. Indeed, when a businessman uses currency as his mode of exchange, he is using something made by the government, and he thereby uses all the machinery of government, its full faith and credit, to guarantee that the paper has the value he supposes it has. Further, taxes are legislated by elected representatives of the citizens, at least in some countries. Since representatives have the right to act for their clients, they can vote for taxes which fall on the clients themselves. Representatives are authorized by their clients to commit them to certain courses of action. In short, taxation is a voluntary transfer of property from citizen to government for services rendered.

This essay fragment has a better claim to expressing a cogent argument than the first. This of course does not settle the issue of which view about taxation is correct. The opponent of taxation might have decisive replies to the objections raised by the proponent of taxation. The point to be made here is that a person's essay will not be cogent unless she does raise and then answer exactly these sorts of objections. Moreover, the position of the tax opponent will actually be strengthened by this process, because it will force him to articulate further grounds for his view that cannot be shaken by the objections already raised.

These same remarks apply to the proponent of taxation. He should explain why there is opposition to taxation, reply to that opposition, explain how an opponent of taxation might respond, and then again reply. Each set of objections and replies ought to be deeper, subtler, and more revealing than the last, if the process works correctly. That is how progress in philosophy often occurs. For more about this method of reasoning, see Chapter 5, section 7, "Dialectical Reasoning."

Exercises

Consider the relative strengths of the propositions within each of the following sets. Which, if any, proposition is the strongest *true* proposition of the set? (Of course, there will be disagreement about the answers.)

1 (a) All empirical statements are based upon observation and nothing else.
   (b) All empirical statements are based upon some actual observation.
   (c) All empirical statements are based upon some possible observation.
2 (a) Lying is always wrong.
   (b) Lying is usually wrong.
   (c) Lying is sometimes wrong.
   (d) Lying is never wrong.
3 (a) Killing is wrong.
   (b) Killing is wrong except to protect one's own life.
   (c) Killing is wrong except to protect someone's life from an attacker.
   (d) Killing is wrong except to protect someone's life from an unfair attack.

3

The Structure of a Philosophical Essay

1 An Outline of the Structure of a Philosophical Essay

Socrates was no friend of rhetoric, as he understood it. Still, he was willing to concede this much: "Any discourse ought to be constructed like a living creature, with its own body, as it were; it must not lack either head or feet; it must have a middle and extremities so composed as to suit each other and the whole work" (*Phaedrus* 264C). To extend the metaphor, just as body parts have different shapes and functions – arms, legs, wings, and horns – essay parts have different forms and functions. Further, just as different animals have different anatomies, philosophical essays have different anatomies. Some are more complex and unusual than others; yet all evolve from a basic form.

In this book, the most basic form and its immediate evolutionary descendants will be discussed. These forms all have a head, trunk, and tail. In prosaic terms, every essay should have three parts: a beginning, a middle, and an end. It was Winston Churchill, I believe, who put it this way: say what you are going to do; do it; say what you have done. You may have heard this before, for a good reason: it is true. Further, as a first shot at specifying the structure of an essay, it is a valuable remark. Yet, this truism would be objectionable if more were not said about what goes into the structure of an essay and how a writer might construct one. What is needed is a more informative guide (given below) to writing.

In the more informative guide, the first element, "Say what you are going to do," and the third, "Say what you have done," are substantially unchanged. They appear below as segments I and V. The second element, "Do it," however, divides into three segments: II–IV.

The Structure of a Philosophical Essay
A Simple One

I   State the proposition to be proved.
II   Give the argument for that proposition.
III   Show that the argument is valid.
IV   Show that the premises are true.
V   State the upshot of what has been proven.

Segment I, stating the proposition to be proved, is the beginning of the essay. The statement to be proved is often called "the thesis sentence," or, more simply, the thesis. The thesis might be a statement like "Justice is rendering each person what is due to him," or it might be a historical thesis like "Descartes's method of doubt is the same as Sextus's skepticism."

Aristotle said, "A speech has two parts: you must state your thesis; and you must prove it." Although an essay is not exactly a written speech, what Aristotle says about a speech can be applied to an essay. The most basic division of an essay is into a statement of the thesis and its proof. The statement of the thesis comes before the proof. If you begin your essay with your first premise, rather than with a statement of your thesis, the reader will have great difficulty in understanding the relevance of the premise. One reason for this is that from any proposition, an infinite number of propositions follows. (It is easy, but not relevant here, to prove this. Anyone who has taken a course in logic should be able to do it. Those without a course in logic might ask their professor, some rainy day, to do it.) Although virtually all of the infinite possible propositions will have an absurdly low probability of being drawn by the author, often there will still be a relatively large number of propositions that have a relatively high probability of being drawn; and it is unfair and irrational for an author to expect the reader to anticipate which of these she might draw.

Compare writing an essay with riding in an automobile. If a passenger does not know the destination, it will be difficult for him to remember the roads he has taken. If, on the other hand, the destination is known, then every left and right turn, every sign and traffic signal, is organized in relation to that destination. Since philosophy can be difficult, it is important to make as clear as possible what you are trying to prove in your essay. There should be no surprises in philosophy, except those caused by an insight, expressed with brilliant clarity. Do not confuse rhetorical pyrotechnics for philosophical light.

Of course, your principal purpose in writing a philosophical essay is Truth for Truth's sake (*Veritas gratia Veritatis*). Another purpose, however, may be to show your professor that you know the material. Before reading your essay, your professor will assume neither that you do nor that you do not know the material; but once he does begin reading it the burden of proof is on you to show that you do know the material. An unclear essay is evidence of unclear thought.

Segments II–IV constitute the middle of the essay. Concerning segment II, it is good practice to set out all of one's premises as soon as possible. This gives the reader the opportunity to see the general structure of your argument. The reader has a chance to see the overall picture of how you are going to get to your thesis. Then, in segment III, show your argument to be valid, i.e. that the premises you have set out will in fact get you to your conclusion. Explain how your premises entail your conclusion. Since a valid argument guarantees a true conclusion only if all the premises are true, the next step in your essay (segment IV) is to prove that your premises are true. First, state your evidence for your premises. This is the most direct and straightforward way of pressing your case. Typically, your audience will be more or less dubious about one or more of your premises. Raising the objections that you anticipate your reader might have will help clear the air of that doubt *if* you can answer those objections. More, answering the objections will solidify your case and make it more compelling for your reader.

Segment V is the end of your essay. There are several ways to end an essay. One way is to summarize your argument. This is in line with the notion "say what you have done." Because it comes at the end of your careful explication, your summary can assume a lot. You may use technical terms freely and assume that the meanings of your propositions are clear. Another way to end an essay is to explain what further implication it has; or you might say what the next step in your research is. This last conclusion is ill-advised if you are submitting your final essay for a course.

Still another way to end an essay is to explain why your results are important, if their importance could not be appreciated by stating them earlier in the essay. Typically, you should explain why your results are important near the beginning of your essay in order to pique your reader's interest. Sometimes, however, the importance cannot be appreciated before one goes through the argument, or the relation between the results and the importance is implausible without the argument. In these cases it is both justified and advisable to explain the importance of your results at the end.

I have briefly described the simplest structure a philosophical essay can have. Typically, the structure of a philosophical essay will be much more complicated. To help reflect this additional complication, let's look at a more complicated outline of the structure of a philosophical essay. See pages 56–7.

The outline is in large part self-explanatory. Still, other things need to be said about it, since it is an abstract and schematic entity. First, not every essay will contain every element of the outline. Second, not every essay will contain these elements in the order in which they are given here. The order given is a standard order, but it should not be considered invariable. Your material should dictate the order. Third, some items in

The Structure of a Philosophical Essay
A Slightly More Complex One

I   Beginning: State the proposition to be proved.
    (a)   Orientation
          (1)   Specify what general topic will be discussed.
          (2)   Report what previous philosophers have thought about this topic.
    (b)   State what is to be proved; state the thesis.
          (1)   Report who has held the same or a similar view.
          (2)   Report who has held the opposite or a different view.
    (c)   Motivation: Explain why this thesis or topic is interesting or important.
    (d)   State what you will assume in your essay without argument.
II   Give the argument for the proposition to be proved.
    (a)   Explain the general force of the argument.
    (b)   Explain what the premises mean.
III   Show that the argument is valid.
    (a)   Explain those terms that are used in a technical sense, or which are ambiguous; resolve the ambiguity.
    (b)   Explain how the conclusion follows from the premises.
          (1)   The inference to intermediate conclusions will have to be explained as part of the complete explanation.
          (2)   Sometimes one can explain the inferences by citing rules from a natural deduction system, e.g. *modus ponens* or *modus tollens*. More often the explanation concerns explaining the conceptual relations between the concepts expressed in the premises.

(c) Give the rules that justify the inferences that are not apparent from the initial statement of the argument.

IV   Show that the premises are true.
   (a) Give the evidence for the premises.
      (1) Explain the premises; and explain the meaning of those terms that might be misunderstood and which bear upon the truth of your premises.
      (2) Adduce the intuitions of the audience; supply examples and subsidiary arguments that lend support to the truth of your premises.
   (b) Raise objections.
      (1) Raise objections that have actually been raised against your position.
         (i)   Raise the objections that historically significant philosophers have already raised to that problem.
         (ii) Raise the objections that your professor or fellow students have raised.
      (2) Raise objections that no one else has raised and which, when answered, further explicate and shore up your thesis.
   (c) Answer the objections.
V   Conclusion:
   (a) State the upshot of what you have proven.
   (b) Indicate further results that one might try to get.

the outline are roughly the same, e.g. I(a)(2) and I(b)(1). One reason for this is that essays typically unfold one step at a time. It is often rhetorically more effective to follow this procedure: provide some general background, then state your own position, then provide more detailed background, and so on. Another reason why the same general topic is listed in more than one place in the outline is, again, that your material should dictate your order, and sometimes that means discussing a topic in one place and sometimes in another. Finally, parts of this outline – even the whole of it – can be embedded as subordinate elements within other parts of the outline. For example, at the beginning of an essay, in the course of explaining what previous philosophers have thought about this problem, you might want to introduce the argument that some other philosopher gives for his position. In other words, you would want to introduce segments II–IV of the "Outline" as an element subordinate to I(a)(2). If you were to do this, then the outline for the early part of your essay would contain embedded elements. (See the accompanying box on p. 59).

Of course, this kind of embedding can occur at almost any other place in your essay, and it can occur an indefinite number of times, even with one embedding within another. For example, for segment IV "Show that the premises are true," the truth of some premise may depend upon some argument that contains a premise that itself depends upon some argument that needs to be explained, so one will need to revert to segments II–IV as many times as is necessary to explicate each premise. Although it may seem complicated to have several embeddings, in fact, it is not. The human brain is quite capable of multiple embeddings of diverse types. If you signal each successive embedding for your readers, they will not be confused by the apparent complexity. The "basic" outline suggests that a philosophical essay contains only one argument. This is not correct, as we just saw in discussing the need for embedded arguments in supporting one's premises. Furthermore, though an essay might have one *main* argument, most essays contain other subordinate arguments which will relate to the thesis in various ways. The author will subscribe to some of these arguments; but in many cases she will merely be reporting arguments of those opposed to her view or "flawed" arguments made by those who will have supported her main thesis. In writing your own essay, you should attempt to show your opponents' views to be faulty while overcoming the problems of previous arguments in support of your thesis.

I   Beginning: State the proposition to be proved.
   (a)   Orientation
       (1)   Specify what general topic will be discussed.
       (2)   Report what previous philosophers have thought about this topic.

> II   Give the argument for the proposition to be proved.
> III   Show that the argument is valid.
>   (a)   Explain those terms that are used in a technical sense, or which are ambiguous; resolve the ambiguity.
>   (b)   Give the rules that justify the inferences that are not apparent from the initial statement of the argument.
> IV   Show that the premises are true.

   (b)   State what is to be proved; state your thesis.
       (1)   Report who has held the same or a similar view.
       (2)   Report who has held the opposite or a different view.
   (c)   Motivation: Explain why this thesis is interesting or important.
II   Give the argument for the proposition to be proved.
III Show that the argument is valid.
IV   Show that the premises are true.
V   Conclusion.

2   Anatomy of an Essay

Printed below is a sample essay, "Hobbes's Divine Command Theory of Morality," which illustrates most items in the structure of a philosophical essay discussed in the previous section. Passages within the text have been numbered [1]–[22] as references to the commentary provided below the text of the essay. For best results in using the commentary, skim the entire essay first (it is quite brief). Then return to the beginning of the essay; read each numbered item and the note for it.

[1] *Hobbes's Divine Command Theory of Morality*

[2] The central problem in Thomas Hobbes's moral philosophy is answering the question, "Why are humans obligated to follow the moral laws?" [3] There are two basic ways of

---

[1] The title is an extremely important part of an essay because, if it is aptly formulated, it helps to satisfy the two most important parts of the beginning of an essay. Since the title is always the first thing a reader sees, even before the author's name, it creates the first impression. The title should convey a narrow range of topics from which the actual topic is selected. This delimitation of the range orients the reader. The title, "Hobbes's Divine Command Theory of Morality," obviously indicates that the main topic of discussion will not include elephants or geological ages. It restricts the topic to the intersection of topics about Hobbes and the Divine Command Theory of Morality.

Of course, understanding the title also relies upon a great deal of background information. The title is more informative to someone who knows who Hobbes is and what the divine command theory of morality is.

[2] The first sentence must effect a transition from the abstractness and sketchiness of the title to the concreteness and specificity of the essay itself. The transition is very smooth in this essay since the phrase, "Hobbes's moral philosophy," in the first sentence echoes two of the key words in the title. Item [2] satisfies I(a)(1): Specify what general topic will be discussed. (The difference between I(a)(1) and I(b)(1) and I(b)(2) is solely in the relation the sentences have to other parts of the essay.) I(a)(1) is a report of the history of the problem without relating that history to the author's own thesis; I(b)(1) and I(b)(2) report that history in relation to the author's own thesis.

[3] This sentence introduces I(a)(2): report what previous philosophers have thought about this topic.

Item [3] is also *proleptic*; that is, it sets forth in a general way something that needs to be related in detail. Proleptic sentences are like implicit promises to say more about the topic. Such promises need to

interpreting Hobbes's answer to this question. [4] One interpretation is that humans must obey moral laws because God commands them to obey. [5] This is generally known as the Taylor–Warrender Thesis. [6] The other interpretation is that humans must obey moral laws because these laws are

---

be kept as soon as possible. In this case, the promise is kept in the sentences immediately following: [4]–[7].

[4] This sentence is the first part of specifying the claim made in [3].

[5] This sentence names the interpretation referred to in [4]. It would be appropriate to introduce a note here that would give references to the scholarly work of Taylor, Warrender, and any other scholar the author thinks provides relevant background to the issue. Such a note is not provided here for simplicity's sake.

Item [5] also marks the place where a discussion of the work of Taylor and Warrender could be inserted, if the author wanted to expand the essay. For example, sentence [5] could easily be expanded into three:

> [5] This is generally known as the Taylor–Warrender Thesis. [5a] A. E. Taylor first presented the thesis in these words: "I can only make Hobbes's statements consistent with one another by supposing that he meant quite seriously what he so often says, that the 'natural law' is the command of God, and so to be obeyed *because* it is God's command" (A. E. Taylor, "The Ethical Doctrine of Hobbes," in *Hobbes Studies*, ed. Stuart Brown, Oxford: Basil Blackwell, 1965, p. 49). [5b] Howard Warrender later elaborated a variation of it in this way: "[According to Hobbes] the reason why I *ought* to do my duty is that God commands it" (*The Political Philosophy of Hobbes*, Oxford: Clarendon Press, 1957, p. 213).

These three sentences ([5]–[5b]) could be further expanded into a dozen or more if needed or desired, preferably by describing their views rather than by quoting them.

Quoting or otherwise indicating what scholars have thought about some philosophical view provides background for the ideal reader and evidence for your professor that you have done research on and are well-informed about your topic. There are many other places in this essay that could be expanded in various ways. For example, see the note to [11].

[6] This and the next sentence complete the discussion of I(a)(2). Notice the parallel structure of [4], which begins "One interpretation" and [6], which begins "The other interpretation." This kind of structure ties together different sentences and contributes to what is called "coherence" or "cohesion" in an essay.

rational, in the sense that they are deducible by reason. [7] This might be called the Secular Thesis.

[8] In this essay, I present an interpretation that is a version of the Taylor–Warrender Thesis. [9] Its claim is that, according to Hobbes, an action is moral when God commands it. [10] But my interpretation also incorporates the main feature of the Secular Thesis, since what God commands is deducible by reason.

[11] Hobbes often asserts that moral laws, which he identi-

---

[7] This sentence is co-ordinate with [5]. It completes the discussion of I(a)(2): "Report what previous philosophers have thought about this topic."

[8] This sentence satisfies I(b): "State what is to be proved; state the thesis."

[9] This sentence partially satisfies I(b). It further explains the thesis. It slightly repeats the information given in [6], but the repetition is worthwhile if the author thinks that the audience might not be very familiar with Hobbesian scholarship. The repetition saves the reader from looking back to see what the Taylor–Warrender Thesis is.

[10] This sentence continues to satisfy I(b). Like [9], it slightly repeats earlier information.

[11] The sentences of this segment satisfy both II: "Give the argument for the proposition to be proved;" and IV: "Show the argument for the proposition to be proved;" and IV: "Show that the premises are true." The argument is so brief and simple that its premises are not even stated in the essay. One consequence is that there is no need to include in the essay anything that would satisfy item III: "Show that the argument is valid."

If the argument were spelled out, it would look like this:

If Hobbes says that laws of nature are divine laws, then
   Hobbes believes that laws of nature are divine laws.
Hobbes says that laws of nature are divine laws.

Hobbes believes that laws of nature are divine laws.

(Some philosophers would claim that [11] does not express an *argument* but only a proposition and the evidence for its truth. I do not wish to argue the point here, and ask that it be accepted as an argument for the sake of exposition.)

There is a good reason to spell out this simple argument here, though not in the essay itself. Some scholars think the argument is unsound; depending upon how "say" is defined, it is either the first or second premise that is false. For example, Leo Strauss thinks that for political

fies with dictates of reason, are divine laws (*Leviathan*, ed. C. B. Macpherson, Penguin Books, 1962, c. 31, p. 399). He also says "The *Word of God*, is then also to be taken for the Dictates of reason, and equity" (*Leviathan*, p. 456; see also *De Cive* 4.1). From the many passages that could be cited, it is clear that Hobbes's adherence to this doctrine is genuine; it was not asserted only once or half-heartedly.

[12] The view that the moral laws must be obeyed because

---

reasons Hobbes, like many other philosophers, wrote words that he did not intend to be taken literally. In an essay as short as this one (two pages), there is no room to discuss Strauss's interpretation or even to mention it.

If the essay were expanded into a 10- or 20-page version, then it would be appropriate to introduce Strauss's views at this point. (For further discussion of this issue, see Chapter 4, section 4, "Successive Elaboration.")

Let's now consider how [11] satisfies item IV. In the first sentence of [11], the author gives a reference to *Leviathan*, which purportedly substantiates her position. In the next sentence, the author actually quotes Hobbes's own words as evidence for her view and also provides a further reference to Hobbes's work. The last sentence of the paragraph claims that other evidence could be provided although it does not provide any of it. The author has presented a fair amount of evidence for the truth of the premise, "Hobbes says that the laws of nature are divine laws." However, in a longer essay, more evidence and some discussion of the evidence would have to be provided.

[12] This paragraph develops a second argument for the author's thesis. Although in theory one sound argument for a proposition is sufficient to prove it, in practice it is often necessary to develop more than one sound argument in an essay in order for the author to succeed in her purpose. There are at least two reasons for this. First, an audience will often not recognize an argument as sound if it is the only sound argument presented for the conclusion. It seems to be a psychological fact about humans that it is easier for them to see some argument as sound if there are several other arguments, even logically independent of the first, that have the same conclusion. Second, an author's audience is diverse. Different people will recognize different arguments as sound. One person may be persuaded by one sound argument while another person by another, depending upon each person's previously held beliefs and principles of evidence. Thus, in order to persuade a lot of people, it is typically necessary to develop several arguments for the same conclusion. To say this, however, is not to encourage an author to present her arguments too briefly or with insufficient detail. It is also

they are commanded by God can also be proven by an argument that Hobbes has to accept. Moral laws are laws. All laws require a lawgiver. There is no lawgiver for moral law other than God. Therefore, God is the lawgiver of moral law.

[13] One objection to my thesis is that Hobbes makes no appeal to God when he deduces the moral laws. [14] My reply

---

not to encourage the author to present as many arguments as she can, no matter how bad or seemingly bad. Presenting a bad argument, or even one that appears to be bad, might be detrimental to the author's goal. Even though an unsound argument for a proposition does not indicate that that proposition is false, it may have the psychological effect of causing the audience to think that the proposition is false. So far as the persuasiveness of an essay is concerned, presenting 20 bad arguments for a thesis might do more harm than simply presenting one sound argument. It should still be emphasized that a conclusion is true if there is even one sound argument for it; and the existence of a million bad arguments in support does not prove that the conclusion is false.

If the argument of item [12] were made explicit, it would look like this:

Moral laws are laws.
All laws require a lawgiver.
There is no lawgiver for moral law other than God.

God is the lawgiver of moral law.

[13] This sentence introduces item IV(b): Raise objections. It is the topic sentence of the paragraph. It invites the question, "Why doesn't Hobbes mention God in his deduction of the moral law?" The question is answered in the immediately following sentences.

The objection is a standard one raised by opponents of the Taylor–Warrender Thesis. Thus, this objection fits more specifically under section IV(b)(1)(a). In a longer essay, it would be appropriate to give a reference to at least the most important of these opponents, and even to describe their objection at some length. If this essay were a draft of a longer essay that the author was composing by the method of "Successive Elaboration," then this would be an appropriate place for expanding the essay in the way just described. Because this essay is brief, even the references to the opponents of Taylor and Warrender have been omitted. It expresses in an unqualified way the general view of the author. This general view needs elaboration, which is presented in the following sentences.

[14] This sentence begins the answer to the objection expressed in [13]. It thus begins to satisfy item IV(c).

to this objection is that it is not necessary for Hobbes to mention God in the deduction of the moral laws. [15] The first step in understanding why this is so is to draw a distinction between the form and the content of a law. [16] For Hobbes, as for any command theorist, a law has two parts: there is its content, which expresses what is to be done, and there is its form, which expresses the authority that obliges that it be done. [17] For example, the sentence, "I command that anyone who borrows something returns that thing in the same condition that it was lent," is properly used to express a law, when it is uttered by a sovereign. [18] It is divisible into two parts. [19] The phrase, "I command," expresses the form of the law; or, as Hobbes says, "The stile of a Law is, *We command*"

---

[15] This sentence continues item IV(c). Although it is not obvious – and it needn't be – from this sentence that the distinction between form and content is a very important one, it will become obvious in due course. It is important for an author not to rush her exposition. She shouldn't try to say everything that needs to be said in one or two sentences; she needs to uncover her thought step by step in neither a hurried nor a dawdling way.

The most important point of an essay should not be introduced as a reply to an objection, for a reply is by its nature a subordinate part of the essay. Nonetheless, it is often legitimate to introduce somewhat important points as replies. If all the replies were relatively unimportant, then the essay would be rather boring to read.

[16] This sentence continues item IV(c). Further, although it begins by relating to Hobbes ("For Hobbes"), it immediately broadens its importance by generalizing it ("as for any command theorist"). The rest of the sentence then characterizes the difference between the form and content of a law. A characterization is always general and abstract.

The next sentence makes the characterization clearer by illustrating it with an example.

[17] This sentence gives an example of what is characterized in [16]. It makes the characterization less abstract.

[18] This sentence begins an explanation of the example. It is proleptic and finds its realization in the following two sentences, items [19] and [20].

[19] This sentence explains which part of the example concerns the form of a law and relates it to Hobbes's own words ("as Hobbes says"). There is a certain redundancy in the information given in [19], but it is justified, because the author's point is not one that is likely to be familiar to the reader and having it explained in two different ways makes the reader's burden lighter.

(*Leviathan*, p. 588; see also p. 317). [20] The rest of the sentence expresses its content.

[21] Although the form of moral laws is immediately clear ("I, God, command"), the content is not. For humans have no direct access to God, since He is invisible and otherwise unable to be sensed. Nonetheless, humans do know some things about God, such as that He is rational. Further, laws must be rational. An irrational or contradictory law is an impossibility. Now, since whatever is rational is deducible by reason, the content of the moral law is deducible by reason.

[22] The upshot of this discussion is that the content of the moral law is deducible by reason but not from our knowledge of the nature of God; and God's command is what makes this content a law and hence obligatory.

---

[20] This sentence is co-ordinate with [19]. But [19] is much briefer than [20]. More, it seems, needs to be said, and it is said in the next paragraph.

[21] The phrases, "the form of moral laws" and "the content" in the first sentence of this paragraph tie this paragraph to the immediately preceding one. Again, this creates cohesion.

Most of this paragraph presents a reconstruction of how Hobbes relates the content of a moral law as rational (or deducible) to the form of a moral law.

This completes the discussion of IV(c).

[22] This paragraph satisfies V: Conclusion. It summarizes the argument of the entire essay.

4

Composing

There are various ways and stages of composing an essay. One might distinguish between preliminaries to writing; writing the first draft; and writing successive drafts. Among the preliminaries to writing are selecting a topic and outlining your essay. Writing successive drafts includes writing second and third drafts and polishing. Not all of these topics will be discussed in this chapter. You can find discussions of all of them in any number of general books on writing. Yet, there is one point that I want to underscore: writing must be done in stages. Do not expect to produce an essay of high quality if you write it straight through in one draft. Too many students think that they have a genius for writing. They are wrong. Fewer people than you think are geniuses and even people with a genius for writing recognize the need for preparing to write and rewriting. Perhaps Thomas Edison was right, "Genius is 1 percent inspiration and 99 percent perspiration." Too many students do not realize that writing is a kind of labor. After Adam sinned, God said to him (Genesis 3:17):

> Because you have listened to your wife
> and have eaten from the tree which I forbade you,
> accursed shall be the ground on your account.
> With labor you shall win your food from it
> all the days of your life.
> And with labor you shall write your essays
> all the nights of your life.

It is tragic that some scribe, cosmically depressed by his fate, omitted the last two verses at some stage of transmitting the Bible, as we know it.

I have spoken at some length and with some harshness about the stages of composing an essay, because neglect of these stages is the single worst failing of student composition: too often students fail to prepare adequately before they begin their first draft and fail to revise.

For most of the stages of composing, nothing needs to be added here since most of the stages of philosophical composing are the same as those of other disciplines. However, there are some techniques of composing that students seem to have special problems with when they try to write philosophical essays and there are some techniques that I have developed and are not discussed in other books. I will restrict my remarks to these topics.

1   How to Select an Essay Topic

The first thing to do before you begin writing your first draft is to select a topic. Your professor may have given you very specific topics from which to choose or he may allow you to shape your own topic from a general one. Since this latter possibility is the more troublesome, I will assume that you are in that situation. Some general topics are:

the problem of universals;
the nature of free will;
the problem of determinism;
the relationship between mind and body;
Plato's theory of the Good;
Anselm's ontological argument;
the meaning of Descartes's *cogito, ergo sum.*

It is virtually impossible to write a good essay if your topic is not more specific than these are. Notice that these topics are formulated as noun phrases. They do not commit the author of an essay to any particular position. For example, the first topic listed, the problem of universals, is neutral between belief that universals exist and the belief that they do not. Essay topics should not be neutral. The author of an essay must commit herself to some position which is either true or false. Of course, an author always tries to prove a thesis that she thinks is true; but whether her thesis is true or false, it must have a truth-value. In order to ensure that your topic does express some thesis, formulate it as a declarative sentence:

There are no universals.
No humans have free will.
Determinism is true.
Mind and body are identical.

For our purposes, it is not important whether you argue that there are universals or that there are not; what is important is that you commit yourself to one position or another. For it will be that commitment around which your essay will develop.

The topics listed above may be appropriate for essays in introductory classes in philosophy. In advanced classes in philosophy, they will be too broad. The more advanced the study of some topic is, the narrower the topics are. One reason for this is that in introductory classes, students know less and have less to say about topics; thus the topics need to be broader. In advanced courses, students know more and have more to say about topics, thus the topics can be narrower. People who complain that professional philosophy is too narrow, do not realize that this is a sign of progress in philosophy. How many of them would complain about the narrowness of most scientific research projects?

2 Techniques for Composing

There are a number of techniques that you can use to begin the process of drafting your essay:

Outlining your ideas (section 3)
Successive elaboration (section 4)
Conceptual note taking (section 5)

None of these techniques is inherently better than any other. The best technique is the one that gets the essay written. Yes, written. If something is worth doing, it is worth doing badly. It goes without saying that writing a good essay is even better than writing a bad one. Which technique is best is relative to the author and to the occasion of her writing. Students write more or less on demand: "Your assignment for Monday is to write a 1,000 word essay on 'The influence of Indian mysticism on Plotinus' doctrine of the descent of the soul'." That's probably not a topic that you would have wanted to write about in the normal course of events. On some topics, your thought may be sufficiently well ordered to allow you to outline your ideas immediately.

On other topics, you may know only that you want to defend a certain proposition and need to elaborate it in the course of successive drafts. On still other topics, you may have nothing more at the beginning than a number of elusive thoughts that need to be written down without being censored by your critical faculties.

These techniques are not mutually exclusive. Two or even all three can be used in the composition of an essay; and two or all three might be used on some segments of the essay, and not others. When several techniques are used, it is not important in what order they are used. Further, one technique can be used more than once; you can use a technique, then another, and then return to the first.

3   Outlining

Outlining serves the same purpose as the "Outline of the Structure of a Philosophical Essay" in Chapter 3. It makes the content of your essay clearer by making its structure clearer. During those initial efforts at composing, outlining can be as helpful for figuring out *what* you want to say as *how* you should say it.

When I was an undergraduate, the culmination of "History of English Literature: *Beowulf* to *The Waste Land*" (a year-long course required of *all* sophomores, engineers and business students included) was the submission of a research paper, 6,000–7,000 words. In addition to the paper itself, all the note cards one had accumulated in the process of research, all preliminary drafts, and an outline of the paper, had to be submitted as supporting evidence. (There were stories about this material being submitted in bushel baskets by the more ambitious students, although I never saw this done.)

The outline was supposed to have been written prior to the writing of the paper. I cheated. Not being skilled at writing outlines, I wrote the outline *after* I had written the paper. I justified this violation with the sophomoric – or was it Platonic? – argument that I couldn't know what the outline of the paper would be until after it was written. Nonetheless, writing the outline after the paper is written is not a bad idea, as a means of checking for coherence and intelligibility. If you *can* write a plausible outline from your paper, then you are sure that it has an intelligible structure. If you find that you cannot do so, then something is wrong with its structure and you should fix it.

4 Successive Elaboration

One technique that my students have found very helpful for improving their writing is what I call "successive elaboration." With this technique, you begin by stating *in one sentence* the thesis or main point of your essay. In trying to formulate that one sentence, you should not be concerned with what your audience might need as background information and you needn't be shy of using technical terms. The required background information and explanation of technical terms are to be supplied in the successive elaborations. For example, you might know that you want your essay to prove this:

Some human actions are free.

Your next step is to build upon this one sentence, perhaps, by supplying the premises that you think prove it:

Some human actions are free, for humans are held responsible for some actions, and persons can be held responsible only for free actions.

Now this essay fragment should be elaborated, and it can be elaborated in a number of ways that are *suggested by the essay itself*. What is an action? What is it for an action to be free? What is responsibility? Not all of these questions need to be answered in the next elaboration, although they might be. Here's one possible elaboration:

Some human actions are free, for humans are held responsible for some actions and persons can be held responsible only for free actions.

In order to understand this argument, several terms need to be explained or defined. By a free action, I mean an action that is not caused by any event other than an act of will. By being responsible for an action, I mean an action for which a person might be praised or blamed. And by an action, I mean any change in a body or mind.

This elaboration suggests other questions and issues: Why is the issue of free will important? Why do some philosophers think that no actions are free? The elaboration of the essay fragment proceeds by trying to answer these questions, either partially or wholly. Notice that the essay, as developed so far, begins abruptly; it does not yet have an introduction. Both the question, "Why is the issue of free will important?" and the notion of responsibility in the central argument suggest an appropriate introduction. Although students often think that the introduction must be the first thing they write and the conclusion the last, it seems to me that the opposite is true more often than not. You cannot introduce a reader to where you want to take him unless you already have a clear idea of where you want to go. Now read this elaboration:

One of the most important issues for human beings is also one of the central issues in philosophy. It concerns freedom and responsibility. In this essay, I will argue that some human actions are free, for humans are held responsible for some actions and persons can be held responsible only for free actions.

In order to understand this argument, several terms need to be explained or defined. By "free action," I mean an action that is not caused by any event other than an act of will. By "being responsible for an action," I mean an action for which a person might be praised or blamed. And by "action," I mean any change in a body or mind that is caused by a motion internal to it.

The biggest obstacle to the view that some human actions are free is the belief in universal causation, that is, the view that every event is caused by some other event.

In this example of successive elaboration, I have added text to both the front and the back of the essay fragment. Often sentences need to be inserted between the existing sentences, and those sentences modified in order to accommodate the new text.

The great advantages of this method of composing are order and control. The method is orderly because every addition is justified and invited by some particular portion of text. The method is controlled because at each stage of the elaboration the author knows what has dictated the additional text; at each stage the author knows what is earlier and hence more basic than other parts.

A student might balk at the process of successive elaboration on the ground that it overcommits her at too early a stage of her writing. A student might protest, "But what if I make a mistake? What if the proposition I formulate as my main thesis is wrong? What if I formulate bad arguments for my wrong thesis? And how could I know my thesis is wrong and my arguments bad unless I first have good arguments?"

My reply is that even if an author *begins* drafting an essay with a thesis that she later finds out is false, and even if she constructs arguments for it that she later determines to be spurious, she has lost little or nothing. For, in discovering that a thesis is false, she has indirectly discovered the truth: the negation of her original thesis. Further, she has discovered some arguments that might lead or have led other people to believe the false thesis, namely, the very arguments the author had devised for her original thesis.

These are not fruitless discoveries. For, if nothing else, the author can recast the essay she originally intended to write in a very simple way. Suppose she originally intended her main thesis to be "unicorns exist." Suppose her basic argument was such and such. But then she discovered that her reasoning was faulty for such and such reason. Then she might reformulate her essay in this way:

It is plausible that unicorns exist. For such and such. However, this argument is not cogent. For so and so.

Often what an author discovers in drafting is not merely that her original thesis was wrong but that it was simplistic and needed some qualification or other restriction in order to make it true. For example, in her desire to refute determinism, a student might first formulate her thesis too strongly as "All human actions are free," and then, thinking that breathing and digestion are human actions, she might weaken her thesis to "Some human actions are free."

Exercises

1 In 35 words or less, state the main point of an article or chapter assigned by your professor.
2 In 60–85 words, state the main point of an article or chapter assigned by your professor.

3 In 140–65 words, state the main point of an article or chapter assigned by your professor.
4 This exercise has three parts:

(a) State the main point of an article or chapter assigned by your professor in 35 words or less.

(b) Restate the main point of the article or chapter described in (a), this time in 60–85 words. This short essay must incorporate the sentences written for the answer to (a) almost verbatim; only minor stylistic changes, such as punctuation or the insertion or deletion of transitional phrases are permissible. Interlacing new sentences between the sentences of (a) is permissible.

(c) Restate the main point of the article or chapter described in (b), this time in 140–65 words. The same constraints specified in (b) apply to this essay.

5 Conceptual Note Taking

The two techniques already discussed, outlining and successive elaboration, assume that the author has a fairly good grasp of the structure and direction of the essay before she begins writing. More often than not, this is not the case. One good way of finding your direction and structure is what I call *conceptual note taking*. It is a kind of uncensored writing and is similar to what some writing theorists call *free writing* and others *brain-storming*.

There are two main purposes for conceptual note taking. First, it forestalls writer's block, which is often caused either by the fear that one has nothing to say or the fear that what one has to say is wrong. Students sometimes mistakenly transform these causes for not writing into justifications for not writing. That is unfortunate. Conceptual note taking undercuts writer's block because it is a process by which nothing that is written counts as wrong. Indeed, whatever is written contributes in some way to whatever becomes the final product, even if what is written is discarded. Moreover, even the thought that the author has nothing to say counts as a legitimate thought to be expressed. Once the sentence

I have nothing to say about the problem of universals

is written, another suggests itself:

I don't even know what a universal is.

And others:

Professor Rebus argued in this way: Suppose a piece of paper called *A* is white and another piece of paper called *B* is also white. Then they have something in common, whiteness, and it is not identical with *A* or *B*. Such things are universals.

Conceptual note taking objectifies your philosophical stream of consciousness, which remains mysterious, haunting, and impenetrable until it is externalized.

The second purpose of conceptual note taking is to provide you with materials to be organized and evaluated in preparation for writing a good first draft. Typically, conceptual note taking does not yield a good draft, nor is it supposed to.

Very often when you wish you could begin to write, you have nothing more than some scattered thoughts on your essay topic. You may have some sentences or examples that you know should appear somewhere in the essay even though these sentences do not state the central thesis and your examples need to be put into the right context. What you need to do is to write down your first thoughts about the topic. The thoughts you have needn't be precise and needn't be complete. You may have only a word or phrase in mind that you will want to think further about and develop later. The thoughts also needn't be in any particular order. At this stage, what is important is getting half-formed thoughts out of your

head and onto paper so that they can be observed object-
ively. It is better to write down the thought that you have,
no matter how inchoate and incoherent, than to wait for these
thoughts to coalesce. There will be plenty of time later to figure
out where they go and how they might advance your argument. You might come to see that you want to hold just the
opposite of what you write down initially. That does not
present a problem. For those initial thoughts present either
something to argue against or the basis for demonstrating
and eliminating confusions others may have shared with you.
Even if you decide to discard those initial thoughts, little or
nothing has been lost. You might not have been able to write
your brilliant essay if you had not traversed the path paved
with your initially obscure thoughts.

Since one of the principal purposes of this exercise is to
objectify your thoughts so that they can be studied, elaborated, and rearranged, it is often helpful to use relatively small
pieces of paper and to put down just one thought on each.
You can use 3×5 inch or 5×7 inch filing cards, or 5×7 inch
or 9×12 inch tablets. If you use a word processor, put in a
"new page" command often. After you have completed your
note taking, it is easy to rearrange these cards or pages into
a more logical order. Ideas written down at relatively distant
times are easily brought together when they exist on separate
cards or pages.

6 Research and Composing

Many essays require some sort of research, some investigation
of the secondary literature, that is, what other people have
written about what you want to write about. The temptation
is to do the research before you begin your own writing, and
you may have been taught that this is the recommended procedure. I do not recommend this, in most cases.

Doing research keeps you from writing, and starting to write
is typically the hardest thing to do; delaying the start seems
most attractive to people. Further, research can inhibit your

writing. If you fill your head or your note cards with what other people say, you may find that there seems to be no room for thinking of what you want to say. Put simply, first write down what you think about the topic; write as much as you can without relying upon what other people have thought. Doing this will force you to think about the topic.

Once you have exhausted your own thoughts, begin your research:

> If something you have written has been written before by someone else, footnote it.
> If something you have written has been written better, quote and footnote it.
> If something you have written has been written in more detail, adapt it to your essay and footnote it.
> If someone else has said what you have said and is wrong, use his view as an objection to yours, footnote and refute it.

In short, don't delay; write first; footnote later.

There is one more case of research impinging on your writing to consider. If someone else has written the opposite of what you have written and is right, then use it to your advantage. For example, suppose you wrote "such and such" and some scholar, say, Professor Wisdom, has shown this to be false. Then your draft can be adapted to fit this pattern:

> One might think that such and such. But, as Professor Wisdom has shown, such and such is incorrect. For . . .

Since you yourself formulated "such and such," it probably has some initial plausibility, or at least is not intentionally a straw-man argument. Profit from your mistakes.

If your writing has become bogged down and you are not able to make any progress, research can sometimes get you writing again. When you run out of ideas or do not know how to go on from some point, read or browse through some books relevant to your topic. Some item in them may stimulate your thinking and hence your writing. It is quite likely that you will need some sort of footnote to acknowledge the help you received from the book if you borrow something substantive from it.

7 Polishing

At some stage, your essay has an introduction, a fully worked out middle, and a conclusion. Before typing your essay in its final version, you need to polish it. There are stylistic burrs that need to be sanded and grammatical gouges that need to be patched before it is presentable. Concerning grammar, I will say only that I strongly recommend it. (There are many books that you can consult for help with grammar). Concerning stylistic adjustments, they are best reserved for the final draft. Although there is nothing wrong with making obvious improvements in style as your composition progresses, you should go through your penultimate draft with just stylistic modifications in mind. There are all sorts of simple adjustments that can be made to improve your essay.

1   Try to find an active, vigorous verb to replace a phrase consisting of some form of "to be" and a noun phrase, especially an abstract noun: "My argument will be" → "I will argue that."
2   Change passive constructions into active ones: "The existence of universals was proven by Plato" → "Plato proved the existence of universals."
3   Transform prepositional phrases with abstract nouns into clauses: "The reconstruction of Kant's argument is difficult" → "Reconstructing Kant's argument is difficult."
4   Use participial phrases to subordinate a thought expressed in a main clause: "Aristotle tried to devise a more naturalistic theory of universals. He came up with his theory of immanent universals." → "In trying to devise a more naturalistic theory of universals, Aristotle came up with his theory of immanent universals."

5 Avoid needless or uninformative qualification: "Plato's position is not really contradictory" → "Plato's position is not contradictory."

6 Reduce complex phrases: "Russell makes use of this construction" → "Russell uses this construction."

7 Make the antecedents of pronouns clear. Consider this fragment: "Aristotle struggled long and hard to devise a more naturalistic view of Plato's theory of universals. This is the topic of this essay." What is the topic? Is it Plato's theory, Aristotle's view, or Aristotle's struggle to devise a view? If we assume that it is the latter, then a suggested revision is: "Aristotle struggled long and hard to devise a more naturalistic view of Plato's theory of universals. This struggle is the topic of this essay."

8 Replace a phrase with one word that means the same thing: "The word *substance* has two meanings." → "The word *substance* is ambiguous."

These are only some examples of the kind of stylistic improvements you might make in a penultimate draft. Different people are subject to different stylistic burrs. When a friend or teacher marks infelicitous phrases and constructions, try to figure out whether this sort of infelicity regularly appears in your prose. If it does, keep on the look out for it. Different people prefer different techniques for eliminating stylistic burrs. These techniques to some extent determine the person's *style*.

8 Evolution of an Essay

Printed below are three versions of a short essay. Because I have been emphasizing argumentation so much in this book, I have decided to make the following examples versions of an interpretive essay, which has as its goal not the presentation of a cogent, deductive argument, but an interpretation or explication of some very brief, but important, passages in a work by Anselm of Canterbury.

Version A is a good draft of a short essay. It should not be

considered a "first draft," but the result of outlining, successive elaboration, or conceptual note taking and revision. Since
only the author herself could appreciate the genuine fits and
starts of her essay, Version A is a relatively cleaned-up version. Only one false start is retained in order to preserve some
flavor of authenticity. Version B is the same rough draft with
some substantive but mostly stylistic modifications handwrit-
ten in. Version C is the final version, the result of incorporat-
ing the modifications indicated in Version B. A good exercise
for you would be to make your own corrections on Version A
and compare them with the corrections on B. You should expect
the corrections to be very different from each other, because
there is an infinite number of ways to modify an essay.

You should think about why certain changes were made in
the following drafts. Many of them are instructive and instantiate advice given earlier in the book. Ideally, these changes
should be discussed with your professor or among several
students. Some of the changes that were made are controversial; you or your professor might disagree with them. If you
do, it is important to explain why and to suggest alternatives. The final version of the essay might be further improved.
How?

A.   A Rough Draft

ANSELM OF CANTERBURY

ON THE RELATION BETWEEN

FAITH AND REASON

At the end of Chapter 1 of his *Proslogion*,

Anselm of Canterbury writes, "For I do not

---

seek to understand in order to believe but I believe in order to understand. For I believe even this: that I shall not understand unless I believe" (*Proslogion* c. 1). This passage is the *locus classicus* for Anselm's view about the relationship between faith and reason. Anselm's view is difficult to understand because both "faith" and "reason" have several meanings. "Faith" can mean either "the evidence of things unseen" or the content of a religious belief. In one sense, the meaning of "faith" is "the evidence of things unseen," as in the sentence, "Someone believes in the Trinity on faith." In another sense, "faith" means a religious belief, as in the sentence, "Part of my faith is that Jesus rose from the dead." Notice in this sentence that *the faith* is a proposition – that Jesus rose from the dead – which might be supported by such evidence as that people saw him after he arose or by faith in the sense of trust in a person. It will be argued shortly that Anselm means "faith" not in this sense but in the sense of a religious belief.

In one sense, "reason" means a certain method of proof, as in the sentence, "Sherlock Holmes figured out that Moriarty committed the crime by reason." In another sense, "reason" means a proposition that is proved by the method of reason.

I suggest that Anselm is not using reason in the sense of a method but in the sense of a proposition proved by the method of logic and evidence.

If Anselm is trying to relate a particular proposition of faith with a particular proposition of

On my interpretation then, Anselm is trying

to relate a particular *proposition* of faith to a proposition of reason proved by a certain method of reason (the method of logic and evidence).

When faith and understanding are used in their propositional sense, they tell us how to complete the phrases, "I believe that _____" and "I understand that _____," respectively. Anselm has not yet told us how to complete those phrases although he has aroused our desire to be told by his repetition of those phrases, as when he said, "I shall not understand unless I believe." We want to know what he understands and *what* he believes. In order to understand Anselm's position, then, it is crucial to understand what the proposition of faith is and what the proposition of reason is. We are told by

Anselm what these propositions are in the very next lines.

Therefore, Lord, Giver of understanding to faith, grant me to understand – to the degree You deem best – that You exist, as we believe. . . .

Indeed, we believe You to be something than which nothing greater can be thought. (*Proslogion* c. 2)

In the last sentence, Anselm tells us what proposition of faith he is going to use: the definition of God being that than which a greater cannot be thought. In the former sentence, Anselm tells us what proposition he wants us to understand: the concept of the existence of God.

Thus, Anselm holds the following view about faith and reason in his *Proslogion* : that he can prove by reason that God exists by using as his premise the proposition that God is that than which a greater cannot be conceived.

B.　A Rough Draft With Corrections

ANSELM OF CANTERBURY

ON THE RELATION BETWEEN FAITH

AND REASON

At the end of Chapter 1 of his *Proslogion* Anselm of Canterbury writes, "For I do not seek to understand in order to believe but I believe in order to understand. For I believe even this: that I shall not understand unless I believe" (*Proslogion* c. 1). This passage is the *locus classicus* for Anselm's view about the relationship between faith and reason. Anselm's view is difficult to understand because both "faith" and "reason" have several meanings. ~~"Faith" can mean either~~

~~"the evidence of things unseen" or the content~~

~~of a religious belief.~~ $^{a\P b}$ In one sense, the

meaning of "faith" is ~~"the evidence of things~~ $^{"nonevidential\ grounds}$
$_{of\ belief,"^{c}}$ $Saint\ Thomas^{d}$
~~unseen"~~, as in the sentence, "~~Someone~~

believes in the Trinity on faith." In another

sense, "faith" means a religious belief, as in
$the\ Christian^{e}$
the sentence, "Part of ~~my~~ faith is that Jesus

rose from the dead." Notice in this sentence

that *the faith* is a proposition – that Jesus

rose from the dead – which might be

supported by such evidence as that people

---

[a] The original sentence is not bad. However, since both senses of "faith" are explained in one short paragraph, an additional sentence is not really required to introduce the two senses. Since it is not necessary, it has been deleted.

[b] A new paragraph indicates a new thought; it signals one border for the discussion about the meaning of "faith" (see note g for the other border).

[c] The phrase "nonevidential grounds of belief" is more descriptive than the original.

[d] The word "someone" is vague and bloodless in this context. Replacing it with the name of an actual person makes the sentence slightly more interesting even though it adds nothing to the logic of the example.

[e] There is no reason for the author to appear in this example. Thus, "my" is replaced with something more general but still specific: "the Christian."

saw him after he arose or by faith in the

I will argue[f]

sense of trust in a person. ~~It will be argued~~

shortly that Anselm means "faith" not in this

sense but in the sense of a religious belief.

¶ *Let's now consider the two senses of "reason" or*
"understanding."[g]

In one sense, "reason" means a certain

method of proof, as in the sentence, "Sherlock

Holmes figured out that Moriarty committed

the crime by reason." In another sense,

"reason" means a proposition that is proved

by the method of reason.

I suggest that Anselm is not using reason in

the sense of a method but in the sense of a

proposition proved by the method of logic and

evidence.[h]

---

[f] There is no reason for the passive voice here. The phrase, "I will argue" is more direct and economical.

[g] Some transition is needed between the paragraph explaining the two senses of "faith" and the paragraph explaining the two senses of "reason." The added transitional sentence has no special elegance; but it does the job.

[h] This and the next sentence go together; so there is no new paragraph. The sentence fragment in between is simply a false start from the first draft, and hence deleted in the revision.

~~If Anselm is trying to relate a particular~~

~~proposition of faith with a particular~~

~~proposition of~~

On my interpretation then, Anselm is trying

to relate a particular *proposition* of faith to a

proposition of reason proved by ~~a certain~~

~~method of reason~~ (the method of logic and [i]

evidence).

When faith and understanding are used in

their propositional sense, they tell us how to

complete the phrases, "I believe that _____"

and "I understand that _____," respectively.

Anselm has not yet told us how to complete

those phrases although he has aroused our

desire to be told by his repetition of those

phrases, as when he said, "I shall not

---

[i] When the author was composing the first draft, she did not know whether the phrase, "by a certain method of reason" or the phrase, "the method of logic and evidence," was better. Knowing that she could decide later during the relaxed period of revision, she put down both phrases without a second thought. As the revision shows, she chose the more concrete phrase.

understand unless I believe." We want to

know *what* he understands and *what* he

believes. In order to understand Anselm's

position, then, it is crucial to understand what

the proposition of faith is and what the

proposition of reason is. ~~We are told by~~

Anselm ∧ what these propositions are in the
         tells us [j]

very next lines.

> Therefore, Lord, Giver of understanding to
>
> faith, grant me to understand – to the degree
>
> You deem best – that You exist, as we
>
> believe. . . .
>
> Indeed, we believe You to be something than
>
> which nothing greater can be thought.
>
> (*Proslogion* c. 2)

In the last sentence, Anselm tells us what

proposition of faith he is going to use: the
                      that   is
definition ~~of~~ God ~~being~~ that than which a

---

[j] An unnecessary passive construction has been made active.

greater cannot be thought. In the former

sentence, Anselm tells us what proposition he

wants us to understand: ~~the concept of the~~ that

~~existence of~~ God⌒ exists.^k

Thus, Anselm holds the following view about

faith and reason in his *Proslogion* : that he can

prove by reason that God exists by using as

his premise the proposition that God is that

than which a greater cannot be conceived.

---

^k The revision, "that God exists," is less abstract than the original "of God being;" a similar change is made again below.

C. The Final Draft

ANSELM OF CANTERBURY

ON THE RELATION BETWEEN FAITH

AND REASON

At the end of Chapter 1 of his *Proslogion*

Anselm of Canterbury writes, "For I do not

seek to understand in order to believe but I believe in order to understand. For I believe even this: that I shall not understand unless I believe" (*Proslogion* c. 1). This passage is the *locus classicus* for Anselm's view about the relationship between faith and reason. Anselm's view is difficult to understand because both "faith" and "reason" have several meanings.

In one sense, the meaning of "faith" is "nonevidential grounds for belief," as in the sentence, "St Thomas believes in the Trinity on faith." In another sense, "faith" means a religious belief, as in the sentence, "Part of the Christian faith is that Jesus rose from the dead." Notice in this sentence that *the faith* is a proposition – that Jesus rose from the dead – which might be supported by such evidence as that people saw him after he arose or by faith in the sense of trust in a person. I will argue shortly that Anselm means "faith" not in this sense but in the sense of a religious belief.

Let's now consider the two senses of reason or understanding. In one sense, "reason" means a certain method of proof, as in the sentence, "Sherlock Holmes figured out that Moriarty committed the crime by reason." In another sense, "reason" means a proposition that is proved by the method of reason.

I suggest that Anselm is not using reason in the sense of a method but in the sense of a proposition proved by the method of logic and evidence. On my interpretation then, Anselm is trying to relate a particular *proposition* of faith to a proposition of reason proved by the method of logic and evidence.

When faith and understanding are used in

their propositional sense, they tell us how to
complete the phrases, "I believe that _____"
and "I understand that _____," respectively.
Anselm has not yet told us how to complete
those phrases although he has aroused our
desire to be told by his repetition of those
phrases, as when he said, "I shall not
understand unless I believe." We want to
know *what* he understands and *what* he
believes. In order to understand Anselm's
position, then, it is crucial to understand what
the proposition of faith is and what the
proposition of reason is. Anselm tells us what
these propositions are in the very next lines.

Therefore, Lord, Giver of understanding to faith,
grant me to understand – to the degree You deem
best – that You exist, as we believe. . . .
Indeed, we believe You to be something than

which nothing greater can be thought. (*Proslogion*

c. 2)

In the last sentence, Anselm tells us what proposition of faith he is going to use: the definition that God is that than which a greater cannot be thought. In the former sentence, Anselm tells us what proposition he wants us to understand: that God exists.

Thus, Anselm holds the following view about faith and reason in his *Proslogion* : that he can prove by reason that God exists by using as his premise the proposition that God is that than which a greater cannot be conceived.

5

Tactics for Analytic Writing

A number of different tactics are used in analytic writing, construed broadly. Seven of the most important and widely used of these tactics are discussed in this chapter: definitions, distinctions, analysis (in a narrow sense), dilemmas, counterexamples, *reductio ad absurdum* arguments, and dialectical reasoning. Since these topics are rather technical, I want to introduce all of them together before discussing each more completely in the seven sections of the chapter (but I will briefly discuss them out of the order in which they are presented in the sections below). Let me begin with dilemmas.

Dilemmas are useful for setting out problems. A dilemma makes obvious some contradictory aspects of widely held beliefs. Since dilemmas need to be solved by some means, some methods of problem solving need to be discussed.

Reductio ad absurdum is one of these methods. It is a way of proving one's own thesis indirectly by showing that the denial of that thesis is absurd and hence false. Since the direct opposite of your thesis is absurd and false, your own thesis must be true.

A counterexample is a way of showing that some proposed solution or thesis is not a correct one; it shows that something is incorrect without showing directly what particular solution or thesis is correct. The method of counterexamples is a method of criticism, not theory construction.

Dialectical reasoning is a way of thinking that can be adapted to a way of structuring an essay. It begins with a simple and

unqualified thesis, subjects it to criticism, revises and refor-
mulates it several times until a complex, sophisticated and
adequate thesis is arrived at. Dialectical writing, which is an
orderly record of dialectical reasoning, is a kind of intellectual
travelogue, in which all the important side-trips are recorded
as adventures necessary for reaching the traveler's ultimate
destination.

Dialectical reasoning can also be used as a rhetorical tactic
in doing something called "analyzing a concept." Conceptual
analysis is the task of breaking down a complex concept into
simpler components, just as chemical analysis is breaking down
a complex chemical into simpler ones.

All of the topics in this chapter concern ways of clarifying
and making essays more precise. A basic way of getting clear
about things is to divide them into different categories, that
is, to distinguish them. Making a distinction often requires
defining one's terms because the terms often depend upon
having a precise meaning.

Perhaps the most basic way of being clear and precise is
to define a word or phrase. The dismissive expression "That's
just a matter of semantics," if taken literally, is highly objectionable. Since semantics concerns meaning, if two people have
a semantic disagreement, then they disagree about what they
mean. And that is a significant matter. (The expression "That's
just a matter of semantics" may have a point if it is used to
indicate that it is not important whether one word or another
is used to express a certain thought.)

1 Definitions

Not every word can be defined. Here's the reason. If every
word needed to be defined, then even the words used in the
definiens would need to be defined; and then the words used
to define them would need to be defined *ad infinitum*, that is,
the process would never end. (The definiendum is the word
that needs to be defined; the definiens is the part that explains

the meaning of the definiendum.) So the process of definition must end somewhere. Granted. But the legitimate question that most students have is when does a word need to be defined?

The short answer is that a word must be defined if (1) it is used with a technical meaning and it cannot be assumed that the audience will know that technical meaning; or if (2) it is an ordinary word used in a nonordinary sense. Concerning (1), it should be obvious that if a word is being used in a technical sense, then that sense needs to be explained. But it is the second clause of (1) that causes most of the problems for students: when can you *not* assume that the audience (your professor) will know the technical meaning of the word? The simple answer is "Almost always." You may think that you do not need to define a technical word that the professor has used because you think that he certainly knows its meaning. Although he very likely does know the meaning of the word, that fact is not strictly relevant to your problem. The issue is whether you can assume his knowledge in your essay. Recall that in Chapter 1, it was pointed out that the student's job is to show her professor that she knows something about the topic discussed in her essay. Consequently, a student typically needs to define any technical word that she uses because the burden is on the student to show that she does know it.

Concerning (2), if an ordinary word is being used, then the reader will assume that it has its ordinary meaning unless you tell him otherwise. Moreover, if the audience has the right to assume that a word is being used in its ordinary sense, then the author has the obligation to use it in that sense.

Here are some examples of how definitions can be introduced:

> The main point of W. V. Quine's article "Two Dogmas of Empiricism" is that the distinction between analytic and synthetic propositions has no theoretical justification. Analytic propositions *are defined as* those that are true in virtue of the meaning of their words. Synthetic

propositions *are defined as* those that are made true by empirical facts.

I shall argue that God is omnipotent and omniscient. *I define* "x is omnipotent" as "x is able to do everything that can be done" and "x is omniscient" as "x knows everything that can be known."

According to Thomas Hobbes, God is neither just nor unjust. *By justice he means* not breaking any covenant; and by injustice he means breaking a covenant.

According to Thomas Hobbes, God is neither just nor unjust. *By "x is just," he means* "x has not broken any covenant;" and by "x is unjust," he means "x has broken a covenant."

It is not appropriate here to describe either the kinds of definition or all of their special purposes. For us it is enough to say that the general purpose of definition is to make the meaning of a word or phrase clear. Depending upon the author's needs, this can be done either by describing the actual use of a word or phrase (*descriptive* definition), making the actual use of a word or phrase more precise (*precising* definition), or by inventing a new word or giving an existing word a technical definition (*stipulative* definition).

Concerning the types of definition, it will help us later to have a brief description of the classic idea of definition by *genus* and *specific difference*. Since these two terms are technical ones, they need to be explained. According to the ancient Greek and Western medieval intellectual tradition, all reality is hierarchically ordered; to know something is to know the kind of thing that it is, its species. And this species is determined by its belonging to a more general kind of thing (a genus) that is differentiated from another kind (another species) by some difference (a specific difference). Consequently, all reality can be categorized by genus and species in virtue of various specific differences. Here is a portion of the classic

division of reality according to this idea, known as the Tree of
Porphyry, after the neo-Platonic philosopher Porphyry:

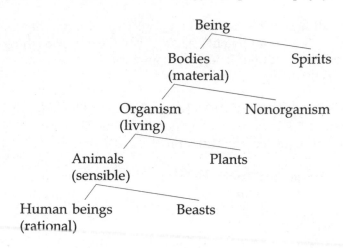

Each capitalized word or phrase designates a genus or species. Each item that is immediately lower than another item is
a species relative to the item immediately above it; and each
item that has items immediately below it is a genus relative
to them. *Being* is the highest genus there is; it is not a species
to anything. Human beings (in the leftmost branch) form a
lowest species; it is not a genus to anything. *Genus* and *species* then are relative terms. A genus is always a category more
general relative to a species. So, Being is a genus relative to
Bodies and Spirits, both of which are species of objects. But
Bodies, to take just one branch of the division, is a genus relative to Organisms and Nonorganisms; and Organisms are
a genus relative to Animals and Plants; and so on. The category of Human beings is a lowest species and hence is not
a genus of anything. (Since this is a division of general kinds
of things, individuals such as Adam, Beth, and Carol are not
part of the scheme. Individuals are said to instantiate or to
belong to species.)

The terms in parentheses indicate the *difference* that divides
one species from another. The difference is called a specific
difference because it, in conjunction with a genus, was thought
to be the cause of the species. Thus, the species of Human

being consists of the genus of Animals and the specific difference of being rational. This accounts for the classic definition:

A human being is a rational animal.

Without a difference, there would be no distinction at all. This issue is discussed further in the next section.

What form should a definition take? Philosophers often deal with abstract objects or at least often talk about objects abstractly like truth, beauty, and goodness. Traditionally, this has led them to try to define *truth, beauty,* and *goodness.* But starting with an abstract noun often resulted in definitions that were stilted or obscure, for example,

To be just is for one person to give another person what the first person owes to the second.

Inspired by certain developments in formal logic, philosophers in the 20th century came to see that many nouns were abstracted from predicate expressions and that the predicate expressions themselves presented more perspicuous definienda. This led to the following changes:

Original form	*New form*
Justice	x is just
Knowledge	x knows that p
Truth	x is true
Promise	x promises that p to an addressee y
Excuse	x excuses y for an action a

Using the predicative form, the above definition of justice becomes the smoother:

x is just to y if and only if x gives to y what x owes y.

By this definition, we know what any sentence like "Adam is just to Beth" or "Carol is just to David" means. One simply substitutes the appropriate names in the places marked by "x" and "y." Let's consider another example: the new formulation of the classical definition, knowledge is justified true belief

becomes

x knows that p if and only if x is justified in believing that p.

And when this is made more explicit, it becomes:

x knows that p if and only if
(1) it is true that p;
(2) x believes that p; and
(3) x's belief that p is justified.

This last definition makes the components of knowledge stand out more starkly than the first.

One last point. It often turns out that philosophers need to define pairs of terms that they want to be contradictories, such as truth/falsity or objectivity/subjectivity (see Chapter 2, section 5). The appropriate way to do this in order to guarantee that the defined terms are genuine contradictories is to define one term and then to define the other as simply everything that is not the first. Here are two examples:

"x is true" means "x is a sentence and x corresponds with a fact f."
"x is false" means "x is not true."

"x is subjective" means "there is a person P such that x can be judged only by P in virtue of P's direct experience."
"x is objective" means "x is not subjective."

2   Distinctions

Philosophy students during the Middle Ages allegedly were given the following rule of thumb: When faced with a contradiction, make a distinction. That rule encourages the abuse of distinction-making and eventually led to the bad reputation of scholastic philosophers, so-called "logic-choppers," "hair-splitters," and "dunces" (after John Duns Scotus). Distinctions should be made only when they are necessary and justified.

Even when a distinction is justified, there are good and bad ways of making it. A good distinction, called *a proper distinction*, has two characteristics: its terms are exhaustive, and they are mutually exclusive. A pair of terms is exhaustive when at least one of them applies to each object of the group that is supposed to be distinguished. A pair of terms are mutually exclusive when only one of the terms applies to each object.

The way to ensure this kind of division of objects is to use contradictory pairs of terms:

red / nonred
blue / nonblue
human / nonhuman
animal / nonanimal
just / nonjust
merciful / nonmerciful

The great advantage of proper distinctions is that they give a neat categorization of objects. There is a place for everything and everything is in its place. This can be seen in the Tree of Porphyry in section 1, above. One of the *personae* of Søren Kierkegaard reports a classification of mankind into "officers, servant girls, and chimney sweeps" (*Repetition*, ed. and tr. by Howard V. Hong and Edna H. Hong, Princeton: Princeton University Press, 1983, p. 162). These terms are obviously not exhaustive, and are not mutually exclusive either. An even more elaborately improper distinction is the one Jorge Luis Borges supposedly reports in his essay "The Precise Language of John Wilkins." In an obscure Chinese encyclopedia, the following distinctions are made between animals: "(a) those that belong to the emperor, (b) embalmed ones, (c) those that are trained, (d) suckling pigs, (e) mermaids, (f) fabulous ones, (g) stray dogs, (h) those that are included in this classification, (i) those that tremble as if they were mad, (j) innumerable ones, (k) those that are drawn with a very fine camel's hair brush,

(l) others, (m) those that have just broken a flower vase, (n) those that resemble flies from a distance" (*Other Inquisitions, 1937–1952*, tr. Ruth Simms, New York: Washington Square Books, 1965, p. 108). I leave it as an exercise for the reader to explain why the terms are neither exhaustive nor mutually exclusive.

While it is easy to see that some distinctions are not proper, for example, red/blue or dog/animal, others are not. Consider male/female. Although it may look proper, it is not. Hermaphrodites have characteristics of both males and females. They are neither one nor the other. We tend to forget them because they are a small minority.

What would be a good way to divide people into sexes? The distinctions male/nonmale and female/nonfemale are each proper distinctions, but each seems a bit odd. Each appears to favor one sex over the other (people have sex; pronouns have gender). One way of avoiding the promotion of one of these sexes over the other is to distinguish between normal and nonnormal sexes and then to divide the normal ones into male and female. (Is it necessary to say that *nonnormal sex* is a biologically descriptive category and neither morally nor psychologically normative?)

A famous example of a philosophical distinction that is improper but has been mistaken for a proper one is sense-datum/material-object. A shadow is neither a sense datum nor a material object. (See J. L. Austin, *Sense and Sensibilia*, ed. G. J. Warnock, New York: Oxford University Press, 1964, pp. 55–61. For another example, see *John Searle and His Critics*, ed. Ernest Lepore and Robert Van Gulick, Oxford: Blackwell Publishers, 1991, p. 141.) Another is the distinction appearance/reality. The appearances of shadows, mirror images, and rainbows are their reality; also the appearances that constitute or are part of consciousness are their reality. (More controversially, the secret thoughts of Zeus are neither appearance nor reality.)

Let's now consider the two ways of drawing a distinction: by characterization and by example. We begin with the latter. A distinction can be drawn by giving enough examples to get the reader to understand what the distinction comes to. Here is an example of an author explaining a distinction by giving examples:

> There are two kinds of labor: alienated and unalienated. The labor of a peasant, the labor of an auto worker, and the labor of a bureaucrat are alienated. The labor of an artisan, a poet and a statesman is unalienated.

The drawback of characterization by example is that it may not be obvious what the principle of division is. Certainly this is the case in Borges's Chinese classification. It is easy for the disseminator of a distinction to be misled herself. If she relies only upon examples, it is possible that the author will conflate two different distinctions.

Characterization, then, is theoretically the better method of drawing a distinction because it specifies the principle or property that differentiates the terms. Here is an example of characterizing the distinction between alienated and unalienated labor:

> There are two kinds of labor: alienated and unalienated. Labor is alienated when the laborer does not have full control over his work or does not receive its full benefit. Labor is unalienated when it is not alienated.

It is often advisable to combine both methods, as in this passage:

> There are two kinds of labor: alienated and unalienated. Labor is alienated when the laborer does not have full control over his work or does not receive its full benefit, for example, the labor of peasants, auto workers, and bureaucrats. Labor is unalienated when it is not alienated, such as that of the self-employed, poets and statesmen.

As my discussion of characterizing a distinction suggests, every distinction depends upon the existence of some property that all the terms of one group or category have and all the things not in the other group lack, even if the author is not able to articulate that difference.

Without a difference, there would be no distinction at all. Sometimes people try to draw a distinction and fail because they in fact fail to specify a difference. This is what is meant by the somewhat inaccurate phrase *a distinction without a difference*. (It is inaccurate because without a difference there is no distinction at all, only the attempt or appearance of a distinction.) For example, in Woody Allen's film *Mighty Aphrodite*, an ineffectual father tries to save face by purporting to distinguish between the head of the family (himself) and the decision maker (his wife). But in fact this is a distinction without a difference. His wife is the head of the family just because she is the decision maker. (At best, he would be a titular head; that is a person with the title of "Head" but without the power of one.) A related example concerns the English Church. When the Act of Supremacy needed to be reformulated, some clerics were reluctant to call Elizabeth I the "Head of the Church," as Henry VIII had been called, because she was a woman. They wanted to make a distinction. So the term *Governor* was settled on. But the Act restored to her exactly the powers held by Henry VIII and the Act described her as "supreme . . . in all spiritual or ecclesiastical things." So the alleged distinction between Head and Governor is a distinction without a difference. Also, there was a tradition in England of distinguishing between the king's two bodies: his physical body and his political body. The rebels of the English Civil War claimed to be trying to liberate the political king Charles I by fighting the person Charles Stuart. The royalists thought this alleged distinction between the royal and natural bodies of their king was a distinction without a difference.

Permit me one final example. A French defense minister once tried to defend his country's decision to resume nuclear testing by in effect saying the following: "The French government is not testing nuclear bombs. A distinction must be made between bombs and devices that explode. The French government is testing nuclear devices that explode, not bombs." The minister was ridiculed, because he was trying to draw a distinction without a difference. But the testing continued.

3   Analysis

Analysis is analogous to definition. Definitions are explicitly about giving the meanings of words. Analyses are explicitly about giving the necessary and sufficient conditions for concepts. Since words express concepts, definitions are the linguistic counterparts to analyses. Much of what was said about definitions applies to analyses. Perhaps both topics could have been treated together; but I think that pedagogically it makes sense to treat them separately.

Every analysis, like every definition, consists of two parts, an analysandum and an analysans. The analysandum is the notion that needs to be explained and clarified, because there is something about it that is not understood. The analysans is the part of the analysis that explains and clarifies the analysandum, either by breaking it down into parts or by specifying its relations to other notions.

An analysis tries to specify in its analysans *necessary and sufficient conditions* for the concept expressed in the analysandum. Necessary conditions are those that the analysans must contain in order to avoid being too weak. Being an organism is a necessary condition for being a human, because a human must be an organism. But being an organism is not a sufficient condition. Dogs are organisms but not humans. Sufficient conditions are those that are enough to guarantee that the concept in the analysans is satisfied. Having ten million dollars of Microsoft stock is a sufficient condition for being rich. But it is not a necessary condition, because a person can be rich without having that much Microsoft stock. Having ten thousand pounds of gold is also a sufficient condition for being rich.

There is one further preliminary point to make. Let's consider this tentative analysis of bachelorhood:

Something is a bachelor if and only if
(1)   it is unmarried;
(2)   it is adult;
(3)   it is male.

This is a pretty good first shot. It is not, perhaps, adequate. One might think that since only humans are bachelors, a fourth condition needs to be added:

(4)   it is human.

However, young adult seals that have not yet mated are also called bachelors. For two reasons it is not necessary for us to argue here about whether or not to add the fourth condition. First, my intention is to give an example of an analysis, not to defend that analysis. Second, what should be noticed here is that setting out an analysans as explicitly as I have just done makes the terms of the disagreement between the pro-seal-bachelors and the anti-seal-bachelors clear. And when the terms of disagreement are clear, debate about what side is correct is much easier.

Let's now consider a genuinely philosophical analysis of a concept:

A person S knows that p if and only if
(1)   it is true that p;
(2) S believes that p;
(3) S is justified in believing that p.

This analysis is very attractive (compare it to the definition of "x knows that p" in section 1). It makes at least one element of knowledge very clear: it is not possible to know something that is false. Sometimes people say that they know something when in fact what they say they know is false. This does not show that it is possible to know something that is not true. It simply shows that sometimes people are mistaken in what they think they know. Our analysis of knowledge also assimilates knowledge to belief. Knowledge is a kind of belief according to the above analysis. This is more debatable. There have been some powerful arguments with the conclusion that knowledge and belief are different psychological states. Again, it is not to our purpose to argue whether the above analysis or some other is correct or not. Finally, condition (3) is surely not adequate as it stands. In order to be a satisfactory analysis, it is necessary to specify what being justified in believing something means. Again, it is not to our purpose to argue about this matter. It is enough to point out that the analysis makes the issues that need to be debated clear.

There are three ways in which proposed analyses commonly go wrong:

An analysis may be defective by (1) being circular, (2) being too strong, or (3) being too weak.

I shall discuss these three kinds of defects in order.

An analysis is circular if the analysandum, or its key term, occurs in the analysans. For example, if one is trying to analyze "freezing," it is a mistake to propose as the analysans "something that happens to a liquid when it freezes." The problem is obvious: If someone needs an analysis of freezing because he does not know what it is, then it does no good to tell him that it is something that happens to a liquid when it freezes. This does not make the notion of freezing any clearer or more understandable because, since the analysans includes the notion of freezing, one must understand *that*, before one can understand the analysandum: freezing. If, on the other hand, someone already understands what freezing is, then he has no use for an analysis of freezing in the first place. In either case, to the extent that the understanding of an analysans depends upon understanding the analysandum, the analysis is uninformative and unhelpful.

However, the above analysis is not totally uninformative. It does convey that freezing is something that happens to liquids, and the person in need of the analysis may not have known this before being presented with the circular analysis. But notice that his informativeness is due to the part of the analysans that did not depend upon any prior understanding of the analysis of freezing.

It is important to distinguish this kind of circularity from a related phenomenon that sometimes goes under the same name. Suppose that we have a number of analyses to propose that have as their analysanda A, B, C, . . . , Z. Further suppose that A occurs as part of the analysans of B, B as part of the analysans of C, . . . , and Z as part of the analysans of A.

Now it may at first seem that someone who did not understand any of these notions would not be helped by any of these analyses. If she doesn't understand any of the analysanda, and each analysans contains one of the analysanda, then it would seem that she cannot understand any analysans either; she has no entry into the circle. In extreme cases, this may be true. Usually, however, someone who encounters such a group of analyses has a fairly good understanding of at least one (and possibly more) of the notions involved. If so, she can get at least a partial understanding of the other notions and also get a better and clearer understanding of the one she started with by going around the circle and seeing how it is connected with related notions. Thus, if circularity is spread over a great many analyses (the more, the better), it may cease to constitute a defect.

This idea of analysis presupposes, however, that the object of philosophical analysis is understanding. Not all philosophers take this view; some regard the object as *reduction*. The idea behind reductionism is that, like scientific theories, one philosophical theory is preferable to another if it requires fewer different kinds of objects in order to explain reality. Thus, if one theory requires one or two kinds of objects, then it is superior to another that requires 27 basic kinds. This explains the traditional philosophical preference for monism and dualism. (The principle that entities should not be multiplied beyond what is necessary is known as "Ockham's razor," after William of Ockham, a 14th-century English philosopher who asserted it.) Suppose that we have a notion of some kind of object, and that it is possible to give an analysis in which the analysans contains no mention of this kind of object. The analysandum is then theoretically dispensable, since whatever we might want to say about it can be said in terms of the analysans instead. For example: It might seem as though numbers must be recognized as existing objects, because we say such things as "Two plus two equals four" and "There is an integer which is both even and prime," which seem to be true only because of certain facts about numbers. But if we can find a way of analyzing the notion of a number, of addition, of being prime, and so on, entirely in terms of the characteristics of physical objects, then we can do without the assumption that numbers exist; for we can say that "Two plus two equals four" is really just a statement about physical objects in a greatly abbreviated form. Similarly, a reductive materialist will try to show that various kinds of things that do not seem to be made of matter, in particular, minds, can in fact be analyzed in material terms.

In some cases the reduction takes more than one step, that is, it depends on more than one analysis. Thomas Hobbes, for example, proposed to reduce all phenomena to motions of material particles. He tried to analyze governments in terms of the actions of human beings, the actions of human beings in terms of the motions of their limbs and organs, and these, finally, in terms of the motions of material particles.

It is clear, however, that a group of *reductive* analyses must never be allowed to form a circle, however large. An analysandum that creeps back into a subsequent analysans has not been reduced away or eliminated from the philosophical theory, and the reductionist's whole project is vitiated. This fact has certain paradoxical consequences. There are many cases in which it is obvious that A can be analyzed in terms of B and B in terms of A, but neither of the two is simpler or more basic than the other. The reductionist who takes Ockham's razor seriously will presumably want to adopt one of these reductions, but he cannot adopt both of them without forming a circle. How is he to choose?

Let me now turn to the other ways in which an analysis

might be defective, namely, how an analysis might be too strong or too weak. An analysis is too strong just in case it is possible to give an example of the notion being analyzed that does not satisfy all the conditions specified in the analysans; conversely, an analysis is too weak just in case it is possible to describe some thing that satisfies all the conditions set down in the analysans, but is not an instance of the analysandum.

Consider, for example, this analysis of bachelorhood:

Something is a bachelor if and only if
(1)   it is unmarried;
(2)   it is male; and
(3)   it is human.

This analysis is too weak, because children satisfy all three conditions, but we do not count them as bachelors; only adults are bachelors.

Let's now consider a stronger analysis of bachelorhood:

Something is a bachelor if and only if
(1)   it is unmarried;
(2)   it is male;
(3)   it is human;
(4)   it is adult; and
(5)   it plays tennis.

This analysis is too strong; it is easy to find bachelors who do not play tennis and therefore do not meet condition (5).

It is possible for a single analysis to be both too strong and too weak. For example, we can combine the defects of the analysis of bachelorhood that was too weak with the defects of the analysis that was too strong:

Something is a bachelor if and only if
(1)   it is unmarried;
(2)   it is male;
(3)   it is human; and
(5)   it plays tennis.

Since there are bachelors who don't play tennis, the analysis is too strong. Since there are male, unmarried children who play tennis and are not bachelors (because they are too young), the analysis is too weak. In short, it is both too strong and too weak.

An analysis tries to specify in its analysans *necessary and sufficient conditions* for the concept expressed in the analysandum. Necessary conditions are those that the analysans must contain in order to avoid being too weak. Sufficient conditions are those that are strong enough to guarantee that the concept designated in the analysandum is fulfilled. The analysis of bachelorhood that left out condition (4) was too weak because it left out a necessary condition. Consequently, the conditions were not sufficient to specify the concept. It is possible to specify conditions that are sufficient without being necessary. Conditions (1)–(5) above are sufficient conditions for bachelorhood. But (5) is not a necessary condition.

It is orthodox to hold that the terms in the analysans are more basic or primary than the terms in the analysandum. However, there are correlative terms that are equally primary. (Two terms are correlative terms just in case the simplest analysis for each term is in terms of the other.) That is, it is incorrect to say that one is more basic or primary than the other. Most alleged correlative terms are contestable. For example, some philosophers have in effect defined the terms *mind* and *matter* in this way:

Mind: no matter.
Matter: never mind.

It is easy to be a dualist if mind and matter are genuinely correlative terms. The terms *particular* and *universal* have also sometimes, though not always, been treated as correlative terms: a universal is something that groups particulars into a class; and a particular is something that is grouped into a class by a universal but does not itself group things.

Some pairs of terms that initially look like correlative terms may turn out not to be. For example, it is tempting to argue that husband/wife constitute correlative terms on the grounds that each is definable in terms of the other:

A husband is a person that has a wife.
A wife is a person that has a husband.

However, while it is true that the concept of a husband is not more basic or primary than the concept of a wife and vice versa, this does not entail that they are correlative terms. Each is definable in terms of something common to both of them:

A husband is a male spouse.
A wife is a female spouse.

4   Dilemmas

Another important analytic strategy often used in writing philosophical essays involves formulating a problem as a dilemma. One reason for this is that one common philosophical project is to investigate and straighten out widely held, but unreflective, beliefs. Many of these beliefs, upon reflection, are either in tension with one another or inconsistent. The same also holds for various beliefs that have been developed after a long period of reflection. Often one view seems to conflict with another view espoused by the same person; or a text is not clear and one plausible interpretation conflicts with a plausible interpretation of another part of the text. In all of these cases, the tension or inconsistency between texts or beliefs can be made explicit by formulating a dilemma.

In Chapter 2, the valid inference forms of constructive and destructive dilemma were explained. These may be called formal dilemmas because they do not say anything about the content of the premises or conclusions. In a more familiar sense of the word *dilemma*, a dilemma always involves setting out alternatives that are somehow conceptually unpleasant. For example, consider this argument, which contains a material dilemma:

If determinism is true, then humans are not
   responsible for their actions; and if indeterminism is
   true, then humans do not cause their own actions.
Either determinism is true or indeterminism is true.

Either humans are not responsible for their actions or
   humans do not cause their own actions.

The alternatives expressed in the conclusion are unpleasant because humans want to be responsible for at least some of their actions and want to be the cause of their actions. (Note that formal-dilemma/material-dilemma are not mutually exclusive terms.)

A dilemma can form the core of an essay. Often it requires no more than an introductory sentence or two and a relaxation of the ascetic style of formal logic. Consider this essay fragment that incorporates the example of constructive dilemma above:

> The nature of human actions is very important to understand in order to understand the nature of human beings. Yet, on the face of it, the nature of human action is perplexing and gives rise to the following dilemma. If determinism is true, then humans are not responsible for their actions; and if indeterminism is true, then humans do not cause their own actions. But either determinism is true or indeterminism is true. So, either humans are not responsible for their actions or humans do not cause their own actions. The purpose of this essay is to argue for a way out of this dilemma.

Although this fragment needs to be worked out in much more detail – definitions need to be supplied, explanations as to why causality precludes responsibility, etc. – it is a start. Because material dilemmas conclude with unpleasant alternatives, philosophers try to resolve them. Since constructive and destructive dilemmas are formally valid, the only way to resolve them is to show that one of the premises is false.

Since they have two premises, there are two standard ways of doing this: showing that the conjunctive premise, composed of two conditional propositions, is false; or showing that the disjunctive premise is false.

Showing that the disjunctive premise is false is called *going between the horns of the dilemma*. To show that the disjunctive premise is false is to show that both disjuncts are false and that there is some third possibility that is true. Consider this dilemma:

> If Hobbes is right, then humans are nothing but
>   machines; and if Hume is right, humans have
>   no substantial existence at all.
> Either Hobbes is right or Hume is right.
> _____
> Either humans are nothing but machines or humans
>   have no substantial existence at all.

It is easy to see that this dilemma can be resolved by going between the horns. The second premise presents a false alternative. The philosophies of Hobbes and Hume are not the only choices. There are dozens to choose from. Good dilemmas are not so easy to defeat. The good ones are usually formulated with a disjunctive premise that either does or at least seems to exhaust the alternatives as in the essay fragment above. The premise "Either determinism is true or indeterminism is true" seems to cover all the possibilities; there is no other alternative. The dilemma might, however, be susceptible to the other method of resolution.

Showing that the conjunctive premise is false is called "grabbing the dilemma by the horns." It consists of showing that at least one of the conjuncts is false. The dilemma in the essay fragment above may be susceptible to grabbing the dilemma by the horns. In this case, this involves showing the first conditional proposition in the conjunctive premise to be false, namely, "If determinism is true, then humans are not responsible for their actions." Someone might argue that although determinism is true, humans are nonetheless responsible for their actions. For humans are responsible for those actions that they cause and are responsible because they do cause them. If this tack were taken and incorporated into an essay, the result might look something like this:

> The nature of human actions is very important to understand in order to understand the nature of human beings. Yet, on the face of it, the nature of human action is perplexing and gives rise to the following dilemma. If determinism is true, then humans are not responsible for their actions; and if indeterminism is true, then humans do not cause their own actions. But either determinism is true or indeterminism is true. So, either humans are not responsible for their actions or humans do not cause their own actions. The purpose of this essay is to argue for a way out of this dilemma. I shall argue that the first premise is false because the first conjunct, "If determinism is true, then humans are not responsible for their actions," is false. For, even if determinism is true, humans are responsible for their actions, and are responsible for them because they do cause them.

There is a third way of dealing with dilemmas: to produce a counterdilemma. This typically consists of producing a dilemma that has the same disjunctive premise. The conjunctive premise keeps the same antecedents; but the consequents typically are contraries to the disjuncts of the conclusion of the original dilemma. The following essay fragment contains a dilemma and a counterdilemma:

> It might seem that human existence is absurd. This appearance of absurdity is tied to the issues of the existence of God, human freedom and salvation. The following dilemma suggests itself: If God exists, then humans are not free to determine their own destiny; and if God does not exist, then there is no hope for eternal salvation. God either exists or He doesn't. So, humans are either not

free to determine their own destiny or there is no hope for eternal salvation.

However, this dilemma does not tell the whole story, as the following counterdilemma shows: If God does exist, then there is hope for eternal salvation; and if God does not exist, then humans are free to determine their own destiny. Thus, either there is hope for eternal salvation or humans are free to determine their own destiny.

Producing a counterdilemma does not in itself refute a dilemma. It does not show that the original dilemma is unsound. It is quite possible for the conclusions of both the dilemma and the counterdilemma to be true. However, counterdilemmas do indicate that the corresponding dilemma is not cogent. One way of showing the lack of cogency is to indicate that the dilemma does not take into account all the considerations relevant to that issue. The above essay fragment makes it explicit that the dilemma does not take into account all the issues relevant to whether human life is meaningful or not. The dilemma records only the downside of the existence or nonexistence of God and not the upside. This shows that the dilemma, though possibly sound, is not cogent.

Sometimes the counterdilemma indicates that the premises of the original dilemma are contradictory. A story is told of a sophist who agreed to teach a student to be a lawyer on the following condition. The pupil would not have to pay for the lessons unless he won his first case. When the student did not get any cases after his education had been completed, the sophist sued. The pupil defended himself by constructing a dilemma:

If I win this case, I do not have to pay my teacher
  (since the teacher will have lost his suit for payment.)
If I lose this case, I do not have to pay my teacher
  (since, by our original contract, I do not have to pay
  him if I lose my first suit).
Either I lose this case or I win it.

I do not have to pay my teacher.

The sophist rebutted the student with a counter dilemma:

If I win this case, my student has to pay me.
If I lose this case, then my student has to pay me
(since he has won his first case).
Either I win this case or I lose it.

My student has to pay me.

The fact that both the dilemma and the counterdilemma are valid and their conclusions are contradictory suggests that there is some contradiction in the premises.

However, there is one more thing to notice about these two arguments. The conclusions are not disjunctive propositions. If these arguments were laid out more explicitly, the conclusion of the first would be, "Either I do not have to pay my teacher or I do not have to pay my teacher," and the conclusion of the second would be, "Either my student has to pay me or my student has to pay me." Since the second disjunct is redundant in each case, it is valid to delete it. This move is canonized in another rule of inference, which can be added to the rules of inference introduced earlier:

Tautology

$$\frac{p \vee p}{p}$$

5   Counterexamples

The method of counterexample is a powerful tool, frequently used to refute a philosophical view. A counterexample is an example of something that goes counter to some proposition or argument. People know how to use counterexamples by the age of five or six. Children often use the method of counterexamples in ways that cause parents to cry. A frustrated parent says to his child, "You never pick up the clothes in your room!" The child responds, "That's not true. Yesterday,

I picked up my shoe and threw it at Mary." The parent is refuted. Sometimes counterexamples induce laughter, even if they are not so intended. A friend of mine had two precocious daughters. The older one once made some slight error, which the younger one pounced on unmercifully. In a desperate attempt to defend herself, the older one protested, "Nobody's perfect." The younger smugly pointed her finger heavenwards, indicating the Almighty. Thus was her sister refuted.

Two types of counterexamples might be distinguished: propositional and argumental. Propositional counterexamples are counterexamples to propositions. Often these are refutations of some universal proposition. A general assertion that all *F*s are *G* is refuted by a counterexample if it is shown that there is something that is *F* but not *G*. The claim that all *F*s have properties *G*, *H*, and *I* is refuted by a counterexample, if it is shown that something of type *F* has properties *G* and *H*, but not *I*.

One of the more famous counterexamples of contemporary philosophy concerns a standard analysis of knowledge. According to this standard theory, knowledge is justified true belief. That is,

S knows that *p* if and only if
(1) *p* is true;
(2) *S* believes that *p*, and
(3) *S* is justified in believing *p*.

To refute this analysis, Edmund Gettier constructed two scenarios, each of which satisfied all three conditions in the analysans above but which were not examples of knowledge. Thus, he constructed two counterexamples. The second and simpler of these went like this. Imagine Smith is justified in believing the proposition "Jones owns a Ford;" (Smith has known Jones for many years; he has always owned a Ford; Smith saw Jones driving a Ford an hour ago, etc.). Imagine that Smith believes it. Further, suppose that Smith realizes that "Jones owns a Ford" entails "Jones owns a Ford or Brown is in Barcelona." But now imagine that Jones has sold his Ford and is driving a rented car; and that Brown, coincidentally, is in Barcelona. Then the proposition "Jones owns a Ford or Brown is in Barcelona" is true; Smith believes it; and Smith is justified in believing it. Yet, he does not know it, because the grounds of his belief are coincidental to its truth.

Although this counterexample is a relatively simple one, simpler ones can be constructed. Suppose Smith has known Jones for many years, sees him regularly, etc. Suppose further that he believes the proposition "Jones is walking across the West Mall" because he sees someone who looks exactly like Jones walking across the West Mall. And suppose that, although Jones is indeed walking across the West Mall, he is behind a wall and out of Smith's line of vision; that the person Smith sees is not Jones but someone who looks, acts, and dresses exactly like Jones. Then all the conditions of the analysans are satisfied; yet Smith does not know "Jones is walking across the West Mall."

One of the funniest counterexamples occurs in a work of literature. At the Mad Hatter's tea party, Alice at one point claims that to mean what one says is the same as to say what one means. The Hatter produces a counterexample to this claim when he says, "Why, you might just as well say that 'I see what I eat' is the same thing as 'I eat what I see!'" (*Alice's Adventures In Wonderland,* Chapter VII). The March Hare supports the Hatter's view by producing still another counterexample, when he says, "You might just as well say that 'I like what I get' is the same as 'I get what I like'." Both the Mad Hatter and the March Hare produce effective counterexamples, because each produces a sentence that is of the same form as Alice's sentence but is obviously false. Thus, Alice's sentence cannot be true in virtue of its form. It is important that the alleged counterexample be obviously false. After the Mad Hatter's and the March Hare's counterexamples, the Dormouse tries his own hand at producing a counterexample to Alice's claim, but fails simply because the sentence he proffers is not obviously false. When the narcoleptic Dormouse says, "You might just as well say that 'I breathe when I sleep' is the same thing as 'I sleep when I breathe'," the Hatter cuts him by saying, "It *is* the same thing with you."

The second type of counterexample involves arguments rather than single propositions. Here is an argumental counterexample involving an immediate inference: one premise and a conclusion. Bertrand Russell thought that the proposition "A genuine proper name must name something" entailed the proposition "Only a name that *must* name something is a proper name." Peter Geach pointed out that this is "a howler in modal logic" (Peter Geach, "The Perils of Pauline," in *Logic Matters*, Oxford: Basil Blackwell, 1972, p. 155). It is formally like arguing from the proposition "What you know must be so" to the proposition, "Only what *must* be so is really known." Concerning this second pair of propositions, notice that the first proposition is true, but the inferred proposition is false. Thus, the inference is invalid; and, because the first pair of sentences exhibits the same pattern, the inference there must also be invalid.

Suppose someone argues:

If Plato was an idealist, then Aristotle was a realist.
Aristotle was a realist.

Therefore, Plato was an idealist.

This argument may look sound. The premises and conclusion are both true, and its form of inference is superficially similar to the valid inference form of *modus ponens*. In fact, however, the argument is formally invalid. This can be seen by producing a counterexample, for example,

If Plato is the author of *The Critique of Pure Reason*,
　then Plato is a great philosopher.
Plato was a great philosopher.

Therefore, Plato wrote *The Critique of Pure Reason*.

Notice that the premises of the argument are true but the conclusion false. Thus, the argument must be invalid. It is an instance of what is known as the fallacy of affirming the consequent. In essay form, the original argument and its counterexample might be phrased in this way:

> It has sometimes been argued that Plato was an idealist. For, if Plato was an idealist, then Aristotle was a realist. Aristotle was a realist. However, this argument is unsound. One might as well argue that Plato wrote *The Critique of Pure Reason*. For, if Plato wrote the *The Critique of Pure Reason*, then Plato was a great philosopher. And Plato was a great philosopher. Therefore, Plato wrote the *The Critique of Pure Reason*.

One of the more famous argumental counterexamples concerns an ontological argument for the existence of God. Anselm of Canterbury had in effect argued as follows:

(1) God is the greatest conceivable being.
(2) Either the greatest conceivable being exists in the understanding only or it exists in reality also.
(3) If the greatest conceivable being exists in the understanding only, then it is not the greatest conceivable being.

---

(4) God exists in reality also.

The monk Gaunilo produced the following counterexample:

(1) The Perfect Island is the greatest conceivable island.
(2) Either the greatest conceivable island exists in the understanding only or it exists in reality also.
(3) If the greatest conceivable island exists in the understanding only, then it is not the greatest conceivable island.

---

(4) The Perfect Island exists in reality also.

The falsity of the conclusion shows that something is wrong with the form of the argument. Since it shares that form with the ontological argument, there must be something wrong with the latter argument also.

Sometimes the nature of the counterexample is a hybrid of both the propositional and argumental counterexample: One shows that a proposition is false in the context of an argument, and the argument is then shown to be unsound in virtue of this false proposition. Consider this essay fragment that purports to present a counterexample to an argument for abortion:

> Some people think that abortion is justified, because a woman has the right to do whatever she wants to with her own body; and having an abortion is doing something with her own body. The argument is unsound. One might just as well argue that punching a bystander in the nose is justified, because a woman has the right to do whatever she wants to with her own body and punching a bystander in the nose is doing something with her own body.

Notice how the same form of argument leads to an obviously false conclusion. If the premises of the first argument are true, then so are the premises of the second. But since the premises of the second argument lead to a patently false conclusion, at least one of the premises of the second argument must be false, and thus one of the premises of the first argument must also be false. It's not the second premise, so it must be the first. Of course, it should be noted that from the fact that the above argument is not sound (because one of its premises is false), it does not follow that there is no cogent argument in defense of abortion. Indeed, it is provable that for every true proposition, there are an infinite number of bad arguments for it. For example, here are just two obviously bad arguments for the obviously true proposition that 2 + 2 = 4:

> If 2 + 2 = 4, then the earth is flat.
> The earth is flat.
> _____
> 2 + 2 = 4

Either Descartes is a philosopher or Plato is a
  philosopher.
Descartes is a philosopher.

$2 + 2 = 4$

Given these two outrageously bad arguments, it should be easy
to see that there are an infinite number of bad arguments for
any true proposition. Thus, a bad argument for a proposition
does not show that the proposition is false. Hence, although
the above argument for abortion is not cogent there may well
be other arguments that are.

In any case, the method of counterexample is often powerful because it allows for a kind of indirect attack on a proposition or argument that could not very persuasively be attacked
directly. It's unlikely that marshaling evidence against the proposition "A woman has the right to do whatever she wants to
with her own body" would persuade many people who would
otherwise believe it. The reason is that it is a commonplace;
it's very widely accepted without argument. (Although it is
a commonplace, it is, I think, false. No one, male or female,
has unlimited rights over the use of their own body.) The principle needs to be restricted in some way in order to be true.
Human beings perhaps have the right to do whatever they
want in connection with reproductive matters or privacy,
or something similar, but not unlimited rights. It is possible
that those who espouse the principle under discussion, do not
literally mean it, but mean something that is verbally similar
to it such as, "A woman has the right to have anything done
to her own body that she wants to." Yet even this principle is
dubious since many states have laws against masochism, self-
mutilation, and suicide. Thus, an indirect assault on the proposition has a much greater chance of success. That's what
the method of counterexample provides.

Although a counterexample is a logically effective way of
arguing against some position, often it may not be persuasive
because the counterexample is not recognized as such. In these
situations, more is required. The author must get the reader

to recognize that the relevant proposition is false, perhaps by suggesting an explanation of why someone might think the proposition is true. Such an explanation is not proof that the proposition is false; rather, it psychologically prepares the reader for recognizing the proof. This has been called "diagnosis." It is analogous to the Freudian maneuver of getting the patient to attain insight into the causes of his neurosis. Diagnoses can be quite controversial; they require a great deal of imagination, and rarely, if ever, are definitive. Different people might believe the same false proposition for different reasons.

Some counterexamples simply refute a theory. If the theory is important, then the counterexample may be derivatively important. This is especially so when the counterexample attacks some central aspect of the theory, as Gettier's did. If the counterexample does not work by undermining a central aspect, it may simply point out that the theory needs some fine-tuning, and that it can be fixed by fiddling with the wording. In such a case, the counterexample is, perhaps, worthy, but not especially important. The most important and powerful kind of counterexample is one that does not merely expose a fatal weakness in some theory, but actually suggests some promising line of developing a different and more adequate theory. For example, recall the counterexample about Smith thinking that he saw Jones crossing the West Mall when in fact he saw only someone who looked like Jones. To many philosophers the example seemed to indicate that knowledge requires a certain *causal* relation between the belief and the evidence, and spurred much interest in the "causal theory" of knowledge. One feature that made this counterexample important to many philosophers is that it seemed to show that there was something fundamentally wrong with the analysis of knowledge as justified true belief. That is, it seemed that the counterexample could not be avoided simply by fiddling a bit with the wording or by adding a more precise phrase (other philosophers, however, did try, and still do try, to fix the original conditions). What also made the counterexample important is that it suggested a direction in which the correct analysis of knowledge might be found. The counterexample indicated that in order for something to count as knowledge, the right kind of causal relation has to hold between the belief and the thing believed. Thus, various versions of a *causal* theory of knowledge were generated.

Counterexamples are a very important method in philosophical argumentation. Sometimes a counterexample can be short and to the point. A philosopher once said that the difference between human faces and animal faces is that animals can't change the expression on their faces (he was thinking of ants, aardvarks, and pigs). His colleague came back in a flash with "What about chimpanzees?" Other times a counterexample takes a lot of time to develop. It needs a lot of stage setting and explanation to show that it really is a case of what it is supposed to be. I urge you to try to use them and label them as such in your essays.

There are no simple rules for thinking up counterexamples. One might say that one should run through a lot of examples in one's mind until one happens on a case that does not fit the proposition to be refuted; but it is fair to ask, "How do you do this?" or "How does one do this in such a way that one ends up with a counterexample and not just a lot of examples that confirm the proposition?" In other words, thinking up counterexamples ultimately depends upon imagination. Some people are quite talented in this regard and others are not.

Exercises

1 Consider this proposition:

> Attending the "Million Man" March was morally permissible even though it was sponsored by a racist (Louis Farrakan) because it was for a good cause, namely, improving responsible behavior in African American males.

Is the following proposition a counterexample?

> Attending the "Respect Our Women" March was morally permissible even though it was sponsored by a racist (the Grand Wizard of the KKK) because it was for a good cause, namely, improving responsible behavior in white American males.

2 Formulate the issues discussed in (1) as argument and argumental counterexample.

3 Recall the passage:

> Some people think that abortion is justified, because a woman has the right to do whatever she wants to with her own body; and having an abortion is doing something with her own body. The argument is unsound. One might just as well argue that punching a bystander in the nose is justified, because a woman has the right to do whatever she wants to with her own body and punching a bystander in the nose is doing something with her own body.

Make the premises and conclusion of the original argument and the counterexample explicit. Explain why both the original argument and the counterexample are valid arguments. Then attempt to either defend the original argument by showing that the author of the counterexample has misinterpreted the claim "A woman has the right to do whatever she wants to with her own body," or revise the original argument in some way that avoids the counterexample.

4 Often famous counterexamples are more complicated than they need to be, and it is valuable to write an essay that simplifies or includes a simplification of such a counterexample. Select some elaborate counterexample that you have encountered in your reading. Try to construct a simpler one that has the same effect.

5 For an elaborate and influential counterexample, read Keith Donnellan, "Proper Names and Identifying Descriptions," in *Semantics of Natural Languages*, ed. Donald Davidson and Gilbert Harman, New York: Humanities Press, 1972, pp. 356–79.

6 Gettier's article generated a lot of interest soon after its publication. The following three articles concern various attempts to fix the analysis of knowledge and additional counterexamples. Read them for further examples of the method of counterexamples.

  (a) Michael Clark, "Knowledge and Grounds: A Comment on Mr. Gettier's Paper," *Analysis* 24 (1963).
  (b) Ernest Sosa, "The Analysis of 'Knowledge that P'," *Analysis* 25 (1964), 1–8.
  (c) John Turk Saunders and Narayan Champawat, "Mr. Clark's Definition of 'Knowledge'," *Analysis* 25 (1964), 8–9.

7 Think of possible counterexamples to these propositions:

  (a) All humans are mortal.
  (b) All humans act out of their own self-interest.
  (c) Whatever promotes the greatest happiness for the greatest number of people is right.
  (d) All persons have bodies.

6 Reductio ad Absurdum

Reductio ad absurdum arguments are frequently used in ordinary argumentation with no difficulty. For example:

> Many people believe the Enemy Principle, namely, that the enemy of my enemy is my friend, even though it is fairly obviously false. During the 1980s, both Iraq and Iran were our enemies. Further, Iran was the enemy of Iraq. So by the Enemy Principle, Iran was our friend. But that is absurd. So the Enemy Principle is false.

Although this argument is easy to follow, people often have difficulty understanding why *reductio* arguments like this are valid and difficulty in understanding *reductio* arguments in philosophy when they are explicitly formulated.

Roughly, in a *reductio ad absurdum* argument, a person proves a proposition by assuming for the sake of argument the opposite of the proposition he wants to prove. The notion of a *reductio* argument exploits an aspect of the notion of entailment. Recall that entailment preserves truth. From a true proposition, only true propositions follow. This means that if a proposition entails something patently false, then that proposition must be false. Now, if that false proposition is the opposite of the proposition to be proved, then the one to be proved must be true. That is the strategy that *reductio* arguments exploit. In short, if some proposition entails a false proposition, then the first proposition must also be false and its negation must be true.

As is obvious from this description of *reductio* arguments, it is crucial to show that the entailed proposition is false. There are two ways of doing this. The surer of the two ways is to derive a contradiction – any contradiction. For example, if you can prove that the opposite of your view of universals entails, say, that it is possible for an object to be in a certain place and not to be in that place at the same time, then it is clear that that view is false; and thus yours must be true.

In formal logic, *reductio* arguments are always derivations of a contradiction. They can be represented in the following way, where $p_1, \ldots, p_n$ are premises, q is the desired conclusion, and r is any derived proposition:

p_1 $\lfloor$ q

p_2

.

.

.

p_n
_____

~q [Supposition of *reductio*]

.

.

.

(r & ~r)

Notice that the premises are listed in one column while the conclusion q is listed at the top right in a half box. The first line of the derivation ~q is the negation of the conclusion. The three vertical dots indicate whatever (valid) inferences are needed in order to derive some contradiction "(r & ~r)." (It should go without saying that the contradiction could be "(q & ~q).") Since assuming ~q leads to a contradiction, it must be false. Consequently, q must be true.

Here is an example that is inspired by an argument of Avicenna:

> There cannot be two Gods; that is, there cannot be two perfect beings. For suppose that there were two. Then one of them, call it G_1, would have a property P_1 that the other one did not have. (There must be such a property because if there are two things, there must be some property that distinguishes them.) P_1 either contributes to making G_1 perfect or it does not. If it does, then the other God G_2 would lack a property that makes a being perfect and hence would not be God. If it does not, then G_1 has a property that does not make it perfect, and in that case, G_1 has a property that is superfluous to being perfect and hence is not perfect.

This argument can be represented as follows:

(1) There are two Gods, G_1 and G_2.
   [Supposition of *Reductio*]
(2) Either P_1 contributes to making G_2 perfect or it does not. [Tautology]
(3) If P_1 contributes to making G_1 perfect, then G_2 is not God.
(4) If P_1 does not contribute to making G_1 perfect, then G_1 is not God.
(5) Either G_1 or G_2 is not God. (From 2, 3, 4 by conjunction and constructive dilemma.)
(6) There are two Gods, G_1 and G_2, and either G_1 or G_2 is not God. (This is a contradiction.)

---

(7) There are not two Gods.

The other, and less sure, way to show that the entailed pro-position is false is to derive a blatantly false proposition. Hilary Putnam attempts to produce such a *reductio* as part of his de-fense that the meaning of a word, say, "water," is not deter-mined by the psychological state of the speaker. For example, if there were a planet ("Twin Earth") exactly like our planet except that the mark "water" was used to refer to a substance that had all the phenomenal properties that water has on earth, but had a chemical composition different from H_2O, then the word "water" on Twin Earth would not mean the same as "water" on earth. Now, since some have doubted this, Putnam presented this *reductio* in defense of his view:

> Suppose "water" has the same meaning on Earth and on Twin Earth. [Supposition of the *reductio*.] Now, let the word "water" become phonemically different on Twin Earth – say it becomes "quaxel." Presumably, this is not a change in meaning *per se* on any view. So "water" and "quaxel" have the same meaning (although they refer to different liquids). But this is highly counter-intuitive. [Supposedly absurd conclusion] Why not say, then, that "elm" in my idiolect has the same meaning as "beech" in your idiolect, although they refer to different trees? ("Meaning and Reference," in *The Philosophy of Language* 3rd edn, ed. A. P. Martinich, New York: Oxford Univer-sity Press, 1996, p. 291, n 2)

But is the conclusion absurd? At least one reputable philo-sopher was not persuaded (Jay David Atlas, *Philosophy With-out Ambiguity*, Oxford: Clarendon Press, 1989, p. 136). So it is not as easy as you might think to produce a proposition that your audience will consider patently false and hence absurd. Consider the seemingly patently false propositions that some philosophers have held:

> Nothing moves.
> Only one thing exists.
> All things are God.

Material substances do not exist.
"Sir Walter Scott" is not a proper name.
Humans do not act freely.

Indeed, inventing an ingenious argument for a blatantly false proposition is the shortest route into the history of philosophy. Consider trying to prove the proposition "Some human actions are free" by a *reductio*. One might argue:

Suppose that no human actions are free. [Supposition of the *reductio*.] Then no human beings are responsible for their actions. But this is absurd. Therefore, some human actions are free.

The problem with this argument is that many philosophers will maintain that it is not absurd to hold that human beings are not responsible for their actions. They may offer their own *reductio* argument that no human actions are free:

Suppose that some human actions are free. Then some events, namely, human actions, have no cause. But this is absurd, since all events have causes. Therefore, no human actions are free.

What is a person to do? Know what the standard of success is. In philosophy there seem to be two competing standards, though in some cases they may not be mutually exclusive.

One standard is that a philosophical conclusion should not, if reasonably possible, contradict common sense, that is, the generally shared beliefs of nonphilosophers. This standard is motivated by the position that the job of a philosopher is to justify or explain ordinary beliefs, not to change them. This is what Wittgenstein meant when he said, "Philosophy leaves everything as it is." Philosophers who adopt this standard have been called *descriptive philosophers*. Of course, it is not always possible to justify all of our ordinary beliefs. Also, there may well be no one set of nontrivial basic beliefs that all people have. Thus, the aim here is an ideal that cannot always be achieved. In the above example, "Some human actions are free" would fit the common sense view.

The other standard is that a philosophical conclusion should not contradict basic theoretical propositions. This standard is motivated by the view that the job of philosophy is to produce the neatest and intellectually most satisfying explanation of reality. While philosophers in this tradition often disagree about what the best explanation is, just as descriptive philosophers disagree about what the content of common sense is, they agree that one should choose one's philosophical principles first and then use them to determine what reality is like. Such philosophers have been called *speculative philosophers*. A special form of *reductio* argumentation has been called the *mirabilis consequentia*. It consists of showing that a proposition "not-*p*" entails the proposition *p*. An elegant case of this is an argument by Bertrand Russell against common sense:

> Common sense leads to science. Science says that common sense is false; therefore, common sense is false.

We can bring out the *reductio* structure more clearly if we formulate the argument in this way:

| To prove: Common sense is false.

Proof:
(1) Suppose common sense is not false.
   [Supposition of the *reductio*.]
(2) If common sense is not false, then science is true.
   [Premise]
(3) If science is true, then common sense is false.
   [Premise]

(4) Common sense is false. [From 1, 2, and 3 by *modus ponens*.]

In an essay, this argument might be expressed in the following way:

Common sense must be false. For, suppose that it is not false. If common sense is not false, then science is true, for common sense gave rise to science. And, if science is true, then common sense is false, for science says that the common sense view of reality is false. Therefore, common sense is false.

Students often find *reductio* arguments disorienting for a couple of related reasons. First, she may wonder how a philosopher can use some premise and then discard it. How can Russell prove that common sense is false when he begins by asserting that common sense is true? The source of this disorientation is the erroneous assumption that the author of any *reductio* argument in any way asserts or subscribes to the supposition of the *reductio*. Russell, for example, does not assert that common sense is true; he merely supposes or pretends for the sake of the argument that common sense is true. So he never commits himself to its truth. He exploits or uses to his own advantage the proposition that common sense is true, without subscribing to it. He offers the proposition for consideration of its consequences; and when he shows that it has absurd consequences, he shows that it is false and consequently that his own view is true.

Second, a *reductio* argument can be disorienting if you think that the author subscribes to the contradiction that he derives. What you must realize is that the contradiction is not the author's. He is reporting the contradiction that follows if you reject his position. Consider this *reductio*, again inspired by Russell:

Descriptions are not names. For suppose they were. Then a name could be substituted for a description if the name and description referred to the same object. Now, since "Scott" and "the author of *Waverley*" refer to the same object and since George IV wanted to know whether Scott was the author of *Waverley*, it follows that George IV wanted to know whether Scott was Scott.

Russell, of course, does not believe that George IV wanted to know whether Scott was Scott. He's pointing out that that absurdity follows if you accept his opponent's view that names are not descriptions.

One final example will illustrate how *reductio* arguments often introduce a proposition to which the author does not subscribe and which is actually the opposite of the conclusion he desires. For example, one might argue that definite descriptions have no meaning in this way:

[1] Suppose that definite descriptions have meaning.
[2] Then "the author of *Waverley*" means Scott (since Scott is the person who authored *Waverley*). [3] Further, if "the author of *Waverley*" means Scott, then the sentence "Scott is the author of *Waverley*" is a tautology. [4] But this is absurd. [5] Therefore, definite descriptions have no meaning.

Notice that the supposition, expressed in [1], is the contradictory of the conclusion [5]. [1] is used as a premise; it is merely supposed for the sake of argument. The author is not asserting or committing himself to [1]. He uses [1] to show ultimately that [1] is false and that the contradictory of [1], namely [5], is true. [3] is absurd. Since [3] supposedly follows from [1], [1] must be false. Thus, the contradictory of [1], namely [5], must be true.

7 Dialectical Reasoning

The word *dialectics* has many meanings. In one sense, it means fallacious or sophistical reasoning. In another sense, it means valid reasoning. Those two senses mark out the extremes of its range of meanings. In both senses, *dialectics* refers to a product: a good product in the case of valid reasoning and a bad product in the sense of fallacious or sophistical reasoning. I shall be using the term "dialectical reasoning," not as the name of a product, but as the name of a *process*, a style or a method of reasoning.

In this sense, dialectical reasoning is characterized by the following:

(a) It is reasoning that proceeds by considering a series of topically related propositions.
(b) Each succeeding proposition usually comes out of or is inspired by prior propositions.
(c) Each succeeding proposition is supposed to be closer to the truth than any earlier one.

These three aspects of dialectic call for some brief comment.

Concerning (a), the semantic relation between the two propositions is paradigmatically that of negation. G. F. W. Hegel, with whose name dialectics is most closely tied, preferred one dialectical proposition to be the negation of the other. However, it is prudent not to take this feature too seriously. Often, one dialectical proposition is merely the contrary of another. (Two propositions are contrary just in case they cannot both be true, but both may be false.) For example, one might move from the proposition that *humans have a natural tendency to do evil* to the proposition that *humans have a natural tendency to do good* and, after examining the deficiencies in both, eventually conclude that *humans have some tendencies to do evil and some tendencies to do good*.

Concerning (b), one proposition comes out of the prior proposition by considering its logical consequences and in that way discovering the limitations of the concepts expressed in it. Succeeding propositions usually arise from one or more of the following types of revision:

(1) negation
(2) expansion
(3) hedging

Negation is the classic Hegelian type of revision. A philosopher might begin with the thesis "Universals exist," and then negate this, in the face of objections, to "Universals do not exist."

Expansion is making more explicit; it is making a point fuller. A philosopher who begins with the proposition "All humans are free" may explain this by expanding it as "All humans are born free although some are made slaves by law." There are many forms of expansion. Qualifying a proposition is one type. Jean-Jacques Rousseau says, "Man is born free; yet everywhere he is in chains." The claim is pithy, but not literally true, even without cavils about his use of metaphor. In the course of his exposition, it becomes clear that what he means is "Man, considered as a creature in the state of nature, that is, not restricted by civilization, is born free; yet in civil society he is always in chains or unlikely to be happy." Qualifying a thesis in this way is sometimes called "nuancing."

Hedging is weakening a proposition. A philosopher who changes "Humans are necessarily two-footed" to "Humans are normally two-footed;" or changes "All human actions are free" to "Some human actions are free" is hedging his proposition.

Concerning (c) above, dialectic has a pedagogical motivation. The systematic treatment of the succession of propositions is supposed to be an easy way of leading a person to the truth. The successive consideration of a series of propositions shows why other possibilities are not correct. This is especially helpful when the correct view is very complicated. A dialectical treatment of a view should reveal why the complicated view is unavoidable. For example, H. P. Grice in his article "Meaning" considers one after the other the following three propositions:

(1) By an utterance x, a person S means that p if and only if S intends an audience A to believe that p in virtue of x.

(2) By an utterance x, a person S means that p if and only if S intends an audience A to recognize that S intends A to believe that p in virtue of x.

(3) By an utterance x, a person S means that p if and only if S intends an audience A to come to believe that p at least in part because A recognizes that by uttering x, S intends A to come to believe that p.

It would be difficult to get a reader to believe (3) much less to understand it, if she had not seen why Grice found it necessary to reject (1) and (2) as too simple.

In a dialectical treatment of an issue, the later propositions are supposed to be more certain and better grounded than the earlier ones. They are more certain and better grounded because the dialectical development has allowed the arguments for a thesis to be presented, the objections to it to be aired, and either refuted or used to improve upon the original thesis. Various sorts of vagueness and inaccuracy of the sort discussed in Chapter 6 have been eliminated.

In one form of dialectical reasoning, one might combine dialectical reasoning with a *reductio*. Consider this essay fragment:

> One might think that *the only things that are real are things that exist*. A moment's reflection, however, will show that this cannot be so. For, if it were, then nothing would be able to change. For everything that changes changes from something that exists at a certain time to something that does not exist at that time. Since what does not exist is not real, by our original principle, change would be impossible. This is obviously absurd.
>
> Thus, it seems that *the things that are real are things that exist and things that do not exist*. Yet this position seems impossible as well. For it likewise does not explain how change is possible: Whatever changes exists. If what changes becomes what does not exist, then it becomes nothing; for what does not exist is nothing. But this is impossible. Thus, something like our original proposition is true. Yet, it must be modified to take the fact of change into account: *The only things that are real are things that exist at some time*. Thus, everything that changes changes from something that exists at one time, say t_1, to something that exists at another time, say t_2.

In this passage, there was a dialectical development that crucially involved the three italicized propositions:

(1)   The only things that are real are things that exist.
(2)   The things that are real are things that exist and things that do not exist.
(3)   The only things that are real are things that exist at some time.

The move from proposition (1) to proposition (2) was motivated by a *reductio* argument, as was the move from (2) to (3). (2) also seems to contradict (1), and to incorporate that contradiction, although in fact the two apparent conjuncts of (2) are not contradictory. (It is perhaps this sort of appearance that led Hegel to claim that reality is contradictory.) Concerning (3), notice that it is superficially closer to (1) than (2). It seems to be a "return" to (1) – with a difference. (3) is more complex and precise than (1). In short, there is a sense in which (3) supersedes (1) and (2); and a sense in which (2) is the opposite of (1).

Here's another example of an essay that incorporates a dialectical method:

[1] All human actions are egoistic. [2] Everyone is motivated by his own narrow self-interest. [3] No one acts in a way that he thinks will be harmful to himself. [4] The current hedonism is evidence of this.

[5] One might object that egoism cannot be true. [6] People who give to charity, parents who sacrifice for their children, soldiers who give their lives for their country, might seem to prove that egoism is false.

[7] Yet, this is not sufficient to refute egoism. [8] People always act out of their own self-interest, even though that self-interest is not immediately accessible. [9] People give to charity to avoid feeling guilty; parents sacrifice for their children for the vicarious pleasure they receive from their later success; soldiers give up their lives, not for their country, but to avoid the shame of cowardice and the inevitable execution for desertion if they don't. (This passage is inspired by Charles Landesman, *Philosophy: An Introduction to the Central Issues*, New York: Holt, Rinehart and Winston, 1985, p. 24.)

There are four propositions that are important for understanding the dialectical structure of this passage. Sentence [1] states the thesis. Sentence [5] tentatively denies [1] in the form of an objection. Sentence [7] reaffirms the thesis in a general way, and prepares the reader for sentence [8], which is a more precise reformulation of the thesis, which is made possible in virtue of [5].

The purpose of dialectical reasoning should be rhetorical or pedagogical. Leading the reader through a number of plausible alternatives on some problem is supposed to make the understanding of the true proposition simpler. The point is to instruct, not to dazzle.

As you become familiar with the writing styles of major philosophers, you may notice that the dialogue form seems to lend itself to dialectical reasoning. The give and take of discourse invites the assertion of a proposition; its refutation; its replacement by another proposition that takes account of the refutation by one speaker and its opposite by another. Each speaker can refute the proposition of the other and thereby lead each speaker to revise his thesis successively. Nonetheless, not all dialogues exhibit this kind of dialectical reasoning. Often the dialogue form is used merely to develop at great length a thesis stated at the beginning and never revised.

A caution should be aired here. Although setting out one's reasoning dialectically is a good way to develop an argument, be careful about trying to use the dialogue form to express a dialectical progression in your own essay. It is a much more difficult form to write in than it might appear. Only the best philosophers and philosophical stylists, such as Plato, Berkeley, and Hume, for example, have succeeded with it. One pitfall is cuteness. Do not substitute cleverness or humor for thought and substance. Another pitfall is digression. A dialogue must be controlled. Although interesting asides and philosophical subplots might be introduced, it is important not to let the dialogue meander or get off course, like the beginning of *Tristram Shandy*.

Dialectical reasoning is helpful for essay writing because it often provides an easy method of organization. In the course of thinking about your essay before you write, or in the course of taking notes before drafting, people often fall into this pattern of thinking:

On the one hand, X
On the other hand, not-X, because of P
Then again, X because of Q
On the other hand, not-X because of R

Students often find this kind of see-sawing frustrating, and they come to think that they don't know what they think or what they ought to think. And this tends to cause writer's block. One way out of this problem is to use the see-sawing thinking to your own advantage. Don't think of it as wavering or uncertain; think of it as dialectical! Use it as the basic structure of the middle part of your essay.

Exercise

Construct a short dialectical passage in which these sets of propositions play the key role:

(a) No human actions are free.
(b) Some human actions are free.
(c) All human actions are caused; but some human actions are not coerced.

6

Some Constraints on Content

In Chapter 2 we discovered that validity and truth work together to produce sound arguments and that to be persuasive a sound argument must be cogent as well, that is, recognizably sound. Most philosophical arguments are valid. Many philosophical arguments are sound. Yet most are not cogent. Why? The answer is that the evidence presented for their premises is either not of the right sort or not presented in such a way that the audience recognizes its evidential force. If a person cannot see that each individual premise in an argument is true, he will not be moved to accept its conclusion.

It would be wonderful if there were some easy way of explaining what constituted good evidence for a philosophical premise or how one could go about finding it. Unfortunately, I do not think there is. Philosophers often use the techniques described in the last chapter – analysis, counterexamples, and *reductio ad absurdum* – but what the correct analysis for some specific concept is, what a counterexample for some specific proposition is, how to construct a *reductio* for some specific conclusion, cannot be described in general and belongs to the substance of philosophy. When people read about or do philosophy themselves, their attention is directed to these matters, and style is not supposed to interfere with understanding that substance.

With that disclaimer out of the way, I want to say something about three issues that relate to evidence: the pursuit of truth, the use of authority, and the burden of proof.

1 The Pursuit of Truth

As much as possible, you should try to ensure that what you say is true. Do not strain to say something "deep" or say something merely because you think it sounds deep. Anyone who can write 1,000 words on a philosophical topic, without saying anything false, much less outrageously false, has achieved something quite significant. Depth will take care of itself.

You will not always succeed. Sometimes you will make honest mistakes. This is something to be concerned about, but not to be paralyzed by. Worry only about the dishonest mistakes. I have already mentioned the temptation to write something false because it *sounds* deep. Other temptations include the desire to write something false because you believe your professor believes it. In the long run, it is better to be committed to the truth than to what you think your superiors believe is the truth. It is also often better in the short run; saying something you do not believe often rings hollow and can be detected by a sensitive reader.

In recent years some philosophers and many students have come to say that there is no such thing as truth or the truth. (I don't really think that they believe this; but they say they do and they may think that they do. Thinking that you believe something that you do not is self-deception.) When they say that there is no such thing as truth, don't they think that it is true that there is no such thing as truth? And if they do, then they are committing themselves to the existence of at least part of the truth. My claim is quite modest. Compare it with what the courts demand: "the truth, the whole truth and nothing but the truth."

Sometimes they claim only to reject Truth, with a capital "T;" but I find their explanations of the difference between truth and Truth either inadequate or nonexistent. Denying the existence of truth is one of those things that strikes some people as sounding deep. I think it is silly.

2   The Use of Authority

People rely upon authorities for many of the beliefs they have and the decisions they make, and often rightly so. It is legitimate to rely upon the predictions of weathermen about the weather – sorry, bad example – upon the judgments of physicians about one's health, upon the judgments of physicists about the nature of the universe, and so on. Yet, what makes this kind of reliance on authority justifiable, is the fact that the authority has good reasons for his or her views, reasons that do not depend upon authority at all. Ultimately, the evidential value of any authority is founded upon the quality of the evidence he provides. It is a mistake to substitute an appeal to some philosopher's authority for his evidence. For example, consider this essay fragment, which includes a misuse of authority:

> Universals are general objects that cause individual objects to exist. Universals either exist in objects or apart from objects. But, since Plato, the greatest or at least one of the greatest philosophers of all times, held that universals exist apart from objects, this must be true and they cannot exist in objects.

This fragment contains a misuse of authority because Plato's greatness as a philosopher is irrelevant to the nature of universals. Many other great philosophers, e.g. Aristotle, held that universals exist in objects. And their beliefs are equally indifferent to the issue. What is relevant is the argumentation that either establishes or refutes the view that universals exist in things. In textbooks on informal logic, an illegitimate appeal to authority is called "the fallacy of authority."

There are also legitimate appeals to authority. It is not possible to prove everything in an essay or even a book. There are circumstances in which an author needs either (1) to presuppose some result that someone else has (allegedly) established or (2) to use some premise in her argument that she cannot prove herself but which has been proven by someone else whom the author can expect the audience to accept as an authority. Here is an example of (1):

> Descartes argues that his existence follows from his think-ing. He pursues the same general line of argument to prove that God exists, that he is not identical with his body and many other things. For the purposes of this essay, let's assume that Descartes is correct. I want to argue that his position can provide a rational foundation for individualism and a democratic form of government.

In this fragment, the author uses the authority of Descartes to provide the assumption she needs to develop the main point of her essay.

Concerning (2), citing the results of an authority can save you the time and effort of providing what requires a proof but is not central to your own project. This use of authority motiv-ates the use of such phrases as, "As Gödel has shown . . . ," which is simply an abbreviation for the argument itself. This use of authority is effective, however, only if what your author-ity "has shown" is both known to and accepted by your audi-ence. Referring to an obscure or widely doubted argument is unacceptable. Also, when you refer to an author's argument approvingly, do not think that you are relieving yourself of some burden and putting it on your authority. Rather, you are taking the burden of that argument on yourself. If your authority's argument is defective, then your argument is defective. (If the authority's argument is good, she of course gets the credit since she devised it.)

While referring to an authority in order to take her argu-ment for your own is a way of abbreviating the argument and avoiding quotation, sometimes quotation is desirable. An authority can be quoted either to express an argument to which the author of an essay subscribes or to express an argument the author intends to attack. Authorities can be friends or foes. A favored authority should be quoted only if the author can-not express the thought any more clearly or briefly than the authority has already done. For if the author can present it better in her own words, she should. Resorting to such quotation then is in effect admitting a kind of failure. An authority can also be quoted if her words have a compelling eloquence. Everyone who discusses Hobbes's views about the nature of man in the state of nature feels compelled to quote him: "and the state of man is solitary, poor, nasty, brutish and short." A quotation might be compelling yet tautologous: "Everything is what it is, and not another thing" (Bishop Butler) or silencing, "Whereof we cannot speak, thereof we must be silent" (Wittgenstein).

A disfavored authority should be quoted if it is necessary to prove that you have presented her position fairly and accurately. It is very important that you present your opponent's position in its strongest or most defensible way, even though you think it ultimately cannot withstand the assault of your objections. To state an opponent's position unfairly is to set up a *straw man*. To refute that unfairly stated position is to knock down a straw man. It is easy to knock down a straw man; certainly it is not much of an accomplishment.

Students are especially susceptible to misusing authority because most of their essays require extensive use of authorities, usually some distinguished and very dead philosopher – Plato, Descartes, Hume, Kant – and they do not know what it is about an authority that is important. What is important is not his fame, nor his admirable character, nor his possibly exciting life, but his arguments. As I have indicated above, in most philosophy the Argument is all. And this explains why philosophical authorities play such a large role in most philosophical essays, those of professional philosophers as much as those of students: great philosophers have constructed great philosophical arguments that should first be mastered, then criticized, revised, and extended. The great philosophers of the past set the terms of philosophical debate, not because philosophers have an inordinate respect for tradition, but because the tradition consists of the arguments that philosophers, made great by their arguments, have devised. As the distinguished historian of medieval and modern philosophy Etienne Gilson once said, "The only thing that belongs in the history of philosophy is philosophy."

In addition to their use of the works of great philosophers, students often have to research the *secondary literature*, that is, the books and articles that have been written by scholars about the great philosophers. Sometimes students are expected to report what these scholars have said, sometimes also to evaluate it. In either case, what is important is the evidence or reasons they give for their views. The secondary literature should be investigated in order to discover whether it throws any light on the primary topic.

3 The Burden of Proof

Connected to the issue of evidence and authority is the issue of who bears the burden of proof in an argument. Roughly, the person who asserts or otherwise relies upon the truth of a proposition for the cogency of his position bears the burden. Recall, however, that it is impossible to prove every proposition. In every science, some propositions are taken as basic and ground-level. They are simply assumed without proof. In geometry, these principles are axioms, which traditionally were considered self-evident. Further, there are many propositions, which, although they are not self-evident, need not be proven every time they are used, since the evidence for them is very familiar. For example, it needn't be proven that the world is round and very old, that humans use languages to communicate, and so on. On the other hand, in most contexts you should not simply assume that only one object exists or that nonhuman animals use languages to communicate. These are controversial views and need support. There are some propositions, however, that are neither self-evident nor supported by evidence presented in the essay itself that might still be used. Sometimes propositions are used conditionally or as suppositions. That is, someone might try to prove that there is empirical knowledge on the assumption that there is mathematical knowledge. In this case, the person would be proving the existence of empirical knowledge conditionally. He assumes *for the sake of the argument* that there is mathematical knowledge in order to draw an interesting consequence of that assumption. Such conditional use of a proposition is legitimate so long as the inferred proposition is not philosophically outrageous. (If the proposition is philosophically outrageous, then the truth of the assumption may be subject to doubt.)

If no science is presuppositionless, it is highly unlikely that any essay can be. The trick is to be able to discriminate between what can be presupposed and what needs to be supported by proof or evidence. There is no rule of thumb about how to figure this out other than by paying attention to what your professor says in class in order to determine what he will and will not allow you to assume. You may need to ask explicitly about whether certain things can be assumed.

You should think about whether your argument needs some proposition that is evident or merely supportable by evidence. In order to refute skepticism, for example, must there be a proposition that is evident, or is it sufficient that there be a true proposition beyond reasonable doubt? In ethics, is anything evident? Do any substantive moral principles, such as "It is always wrong intentionally to say what is false" or "It is always wrong to appropriate the property of another person," need to be evident or is it sufficient that they be more reasonable than any competing principle? These continue to be controversial philosophical questions, and how you answer them will largely determine the type of argument you will need to construct in order to support the thesis of your essay.

7

Some Goals of Form

Essays ought to be intelligible to the reader. If you have a great argument and cannot communicate it to your reader, then it has no practical value. Three of the most important ways to make your essay intelligible are to make sure that it is clear, concise, and coherent. Philosophers also strive for what they call "rigor." These four qualities are the topic of this chapter.

1 Coherence

One of the most serious failings in an essay is incoherence, which is not the same as meaninglessness. Meaninglessness, as I want to use the word, is an absolute notion. A sentence is either meaningless or not, and it cannot be made intelligible simply by putting it in some context. Coherence, by contrast, is relative. A sentence that is perfectly meaningful in itself might be incoherent within the context of an essay. For example, the sentence "Kant is the author of *The Critique of Pure Reason*" is certainly meaningful in itself and not difficult to understand; yet in some contexts it would be incoherent, as in this essay fragment:

Plato, who is the greatest of the ancient Greek philosophers, wondered how it could be that many different things could all belong to the same kind. Kant is the author of *The Critique of Pure Reason*. Given that Fido, Bowser, and Spuds are all dogs, they are in some way the same. What makes them the same?

The sentence about Kant is so out of place in this fragment that one might be tempted to say of it that it makes no sense or even that it is meaningless. But I am emphasizing that it does not lack sense and is not meaningless but only incoherent in certain contexts. A sentence is incoherent when it does not hang together with its immediately preceding or succeeding sentence. A paragraph is incoherent when it does not hang together with its immediately preceding or succeeding paragraph. And an essay is incoherent when a large number of its sentences or paragraphs are incoherent.

A large part of coherence is continuity, that is, the way an essay moves from one part to another toward its goal. An essay that meanders, seemingly not directed to any particular destination, is defective even if each sentence is charged with great rhetorical energy.

There are many ways in which coherence is achieved in essays. Sometimes one part of an essay coheres with another because they share a subject matter, as in this essay fragment:

Plato holds that universals really exist. Universals then are part of the ultimate furniture of the world. If there were no universals then nothing else could exist.

Each sentence in this fragment is held together by its shared subject matter: universals.

In addition to sharing a specific subject matter, sentences hang together in other ways. One of these ways is through stock phrases that mark the boundaries of large parts of the essay: the beginning, the middle, and the end. Consider these:

I begin/To begin
I shall now argue/Consider the argument
I conclude/To conclude/In conclusion

Even if these phrases are not particularly elegant, they are effective for informing the reader of where he is in the essay, and all three together tie the large structural units of the essay together into a whole.

Other linguistic devices connect smaller portions of essays, one paragraph to another, one sentence to another, and even one part of a sentence to another part of the same sentence. Such devices are often called *transitional phrases*. Their effect is much more local than phrases like, "I begin," "In conclusion," and "I shall argue," which control relatively large portions of text. Most of the linguistic devices available for tying essay parts together occur in the middle of an essay, where most of the twists and turns of the argument occur. The author needs to supply her reader with road signs marking where the subarguments are introduced and objections are raised and answered. One good place for these road signs is at the beginning of paragraphs. For example, consider the opening phrases of six successive paragraphs from Charles Landesman's *Philosophy: An Introduction to the Central Issues*:

> An argument against hedonism was developed by G. E. Moore . . .
> The hedonist has two responses to Moore. First, . . . Second, . . .
> Another argument against hedonism . . .
> The hedonist replies . . .
> Thus hedonism is not refuted . . .

At the very beginning, Landesman makes clear what the main topic of each of these paragraphs is. The reader should be grateful to the author for keeping him informed of where he is in the essay. Your professor will be similarly grateful – and may well express his gratitude in the way you like best – if you use similar types of transitional phrases.

Here is another example of transitional phrases at the beginning of successive paragraphs:

> We shall begin our consideration of empiricism by turning to Locke.

One might object to Locke's empiricism by pointing out
　　that . . .
There is a twofold reply to this objection.
The objector, however, might not accept this reply on the
　　grounds that . . .

In addition to transitional devices that begin paragraphs, there
are also transitional words and phrases that are useful within
paragraphs. The words *therefore* and *consequently* indicate the
conclusion of an argument, often wholly within a paragraph.
The words *further, furthermore, moreover,* and *in addition* indicate that additional evidence or information about some matter will be provided.

Pronouns and nominalizations can also be used to effect
coherence. Compare these two sequences:

Plato argues that the nature of justice is more easily
observed in the state than it is in the individual. Plato uses
the premise that what is larger is more easily observed.

Plato argues that the nature of justice is more easily
observed in the state than it is in the individual. His argument uses the premise that what is larger is more easily
observed.

Both passages express the same information. Yet the second
coheres in a way that the first does not. The coherence is
achieved by the use of two words: *his* and *argument*. The pronoun *his* requires the reader to find its antecedent, which is in
the prior sentence. Similarly, the abstract noun "argument,"
formed from the verb "argue," requires the reader to find
its antecedent, which is also in the preceding sentence. So,
although abstract words should not be used for their own
sake, there are reasons for using them and one of them is
coherence. Here are three more examples of having one sentence cohere better with another by changing a verb from one
sentence into an abstract noun and using it in the following
sentence:

Thrasymachus proposes that justice is what serves the strong. His proposition is refuted by Socrates.

Camus recommends that we choose our values. His recommendation is a good one.

Heidegger challenges contemporary philosophers to return to the roots of philosophy. His challenge has been met in unexpected ways by Derrida.

Virtually all the principles and devices for achieving coherence in an essay that I have mentioned should be familiar to you from courses in composition. What I have tried to do is to make you aware that those general principles and devices apply to philosophy as well and to try to move you to use the available devices in your own philosophical prose.

Exercises

1 Find and write out three successive paragraphs from some philosophical work that contain explicit transitional phrases at the beginning of each paragraph.
2 Think of ten transitional words or phrases that might appear in essays. (Hint: look at some essays for examples.)

2 Clarity

It is quite possible for an essay to be coherent but not clear. Each sentence might be obviously tied to every other without any of the sentences conveying the author's thought:

Art challenges the prevailing principle of reason: in representing the order of sensuousness, it invokes a tabooed logic – the logic of gratification as against that of repression. Behind the sublimated aesthetic form, the unsublimated content shows forth: the commitment of art to the pleasure principle. The investigation of the erotic roots of art plays a large role in psychoanalysis. (Herbert Marcuse, *Eros and Civilization*, New York: Vintage Books, 1955, pp. 168–9)

There is coherence here; but not, I think, clarity. Marcuse could have made roughly the same claims in this way:

> Art is as important to life as reason although philosophers have often overlooked this fact. Art is primarily concerned with the satisfactions of sensuous experience. Even when constrained by specific artistic forms, the sensuousness of art can still be perceived. A large part of psychoanalysis has been devoted to investigating the sensuous satisfactions that come from art.

It is slightly embarrassing for a philosopher to preach about clarity, because so much philosophical writing lacks that quality. Nonetheless, clarity remains an ideal. Wittgenstein wrote, "Whatever can be said can be said clearly" (*Tractatus Logico-Philosophicus*). Schopenhauer wrote, "The real philosopher will always look for clearness and distinctness; he will invariably try to resemble not a turbid, impetuous torrent, but rather a Swiss lake which by its calm combines great depth with great clearness, the depth revealing itself precisely through its clearness" (quoted by Peter A. French, "Toward the Headwaters of Philosophy: Curriculum Revision at Trinity University," in *Proceedings and Addresses of the American Philosophical Association* 58 (1985), p. 615). Joseph Butler wrote, "Confusion and Perplexity in Writing is indeed without excuse, because anyone may, if he pleases, know whether he understands and sees through what he is about" (Joseph Butler, *Five Sermons*, Indianapolis: Hackett, 1983, p. 12). Butler may have overstated the truth; perhaps an author does not *always* know that his writing is confusing, especially when he understands his material thoroughly. Nonetheless, what Butler meant is true in very many cases. Further, just because it is likely that an author might not know that his writing is confused unless he thinks about that very possibility with some care, it is all the more important that he do so. For what Butler says immediately after the passage above is right: "and it is unpardonable for a man to lay his thought before others when he is conscious that he himself does not know whereabouts he is, or how the matter before him stands" (Butler, *Five Sermons*, p. 12). There is no excuse for a person who intentionally writes in a confused way. Authors have an obligation to be clear.

Clarity is relative to an audience. What is clear to one person at one time in one situation might not be clear to another person at another time in another situation. What counts as a clear exposition of Gödel's incompleteness theorem for a Harvard logician might not count as a clear exposition for a person taking his first course in philosophy. Whether writing is clear or not depends in part upon what facts or beliefs the author can rightfully presuppose that his audience possesses.

How many times have you heard people say in frustration, "Well, you know what I mean," when they have repeatedly failed to say what they mean about the most ordinary sorts of things. Think about how much more difficult it is to say something *exactly* right about the most central, important, and elusive of our concepts when no one has previously said it exactly right. In philosophy, after failing to say something correctly, it is never acceptable to fall back on the phrase, "Well, you know what I mean." If the audience knows what the author means without him saying it correctly, then it is trivial; and if it is not trivial, the audience cannot be sure of what the author means.

It is easy to say "Be clear" and difficult to say what clarity is. In the broad sense in which I am using the term, clarity is a complex concept with many dimensions. In philosophy, the dimension that stands out most of all is precision. Precision avoids three things: ambiguity, vagueness, and indeterminateness.

An ambiguous word, phrase, or sentence is one that has two or more meanings. The sentence "Mary went to the bank" is ambiguous between "Mary went to the financial institution" and "Mary went to the river's edge." Although it is highly unlikely that the sentence just considered would cause any philosophical confusion, there are ambiguous sentences that have, and calling attention to the ambiguities involved in them constitutes philosophical progress. Psychological egoism holds to this proposition: Every person acts only to satisfy his own desires. This sentence seems at once both obviously true and outrageous. How is this possible? It is possible because it is ambiguous. In one sense it means, "Everything a person does is something that he wants to do." In order to act a person must be moved by something to act, and this thing that moves a person is called a *want* or a *desire*. This is true and not very exciting; many would consider it trivial. In another sense the thesis of psychological egoism means, "Every person acts only to satisfy his own desires and no one else's." This makes psychological egoism outrageous and false. Gandhi, Martin Luther King, Jr, and Mother Theresa are three indubitable examples of people who, although they did what they wanted to do, were also moved to do things to satisfy the desires of other people and only for the good of those other people. That is what they desired. When the trivially true sense of the thesis of psychological egoism is conflated with the outrageous and false sense, the thesis seems compelling and profound. Psychological egoism trades on this ambiguity. (See Hastings Rashdall, *Theory of Good and Evil*, Oxford: Clarendon Press, 1907.) Once the ambiguity of the thesis is pointed out, psychological egoism is not persuasive.

Ambiguity should not be conflated with vagueness:

Parent: Where are you going?
Teenager: Out.
Parent: What are you going to do?
Teenager: This and that.

The teenager's answers are vague, not ambiguous. They lack specificity. Writers are often vague when they do not know how to formulate their thought precisely although there is a precise formulation of it. Vagueness should ultimately be eliminated in these cases. What this means is that you should work to eliminate unnecessarily vague words and sentences. This is not to say that vagueness should not occur in the early drafts of your essay. To the contrary, this is a good place for it. When you are first working out your thoughts, write down whatever comes to mind. Many of these things will be vague. That is okay. After you have written your initial thoughts, revise. Eliminate the vagueness by reflecting more carefully on the issue; also use a dictionary and thesaurus to help you find the precise word that you want.

So far I have been talking about avoidable vagueness. Some vagueness is unavoidable. Some phenomena lack sharp boundaries by their very nature; and they would be misrepresented if overly specific language were used to describe them. One importantly vague concept may be the ordinary concept of a person. Suppose that two people, Sharp and Blunt, are operated on and their brains interchanged. After the operation, which person is Sharp and which is Blunt? If you think that the obvious answer to this question is that Mr Blunt is the object consisting of Blunt's brain in Sharp's body and Mr Sharp is the object consisting of Sharp's brain in Blunt's body (on the grounds that whoever has a person's brain is that person), then consider a related, though different, situation. Suppose that Sharp and Blunt are operated on; their brains are interchanged. However, in the course of the interchange, all the brain states of each brain are also interchanged. That is, all the original states of Sharp's brain are now encoded in Blunt's brain, and all the original states of Blunt's brain are now encoded in Sharp's brain. In this situation, Sharp's body has Blunt's brain but Sharp's brain states; and Blunt's body has Sharp's brain but has Blunt's brain states. Now which object is Sharp and which Blunt? People might well argue about which is the right answer. Another way to handle the question, however, is to claim that there is no *right* answer, because the concept of a person is not so definite as to allow an answer to this question. The situation is so bizarre that a solution to it has never been built into the ordinary concept of a person. Now nothing prevents us from adding to that original concept something that does determine the answer.

Only be aware that in adding to that concept, we are thereby changing it, and, more precisely, are admitting that the original concept had some degree of vagueness.

The point of all this is that some vagueness is built into some concepts and that it is not a defect when your writing reflects this vagueness. However, it is important to be aware of this vagueness. As Aristotle said, "It is the mark of an educated person not to require more precision than the subject allows." (See Wittgenstein, *Philosophical Investigations*, for more about precision and exactness.)

In addition to the avoidable vagueness that is objectionable in philosophy, and the unavoidable vagueness that is to be recommended, there is a third category, that of avoidable vagueness that is to be recommended. This is a kind of vagueness that is put to work in the service of style. Often, especially when a topic is difficult or when what is to be said about the topic is quite original, a precise formulation of one's views, though intelligible in itself, might be relatively unintelligible to an unprepared reader. In such cases, it is often rhetorically advisable to begin with a vague statement of one's position and use it as the occasion to invite a more precise formulation of it. For example, John Searle had astonishingly original things to say about intentionality in his book *Intentionality*, most of which, when formulated precisely, were unavoidably couched in technical terms. Such terms would have been unintelligible to his readers early in the book. Thus, as a first shot at explaining his views, Searle writes:

> All of these . . . connections between Intentional states and speech acts naturally suggest a certain picture of Intentionality: every Intentional state consists of a representative content in a certain psychological mode. Intentional states represent objects and states of affairs. . . . Just as my statement that it is raining is a representation of a certain state of affairs, so my belief that it is raining is a representation of the same state of affairs. Just as my order to Sam to leave the room is about Sam and represents a certain action on his part, so my desire that Sam

should leave the room is about Sam and represents a certain action on his part. (*Intentionality*, Cambridge: Cambridge University Press, 1983, p. 11)

Searle's use of "represent" and "representation" helps establish a context that is familiar to philosophers. Yet philosophers
have rarely, if ever, spelled out what a representation is. Searle
is aware of this vagueness and is exploiting it. He goes on to
say, "The notion of representation is conveniently vague." He
admits to "Exploiting this vagueness," and acknowledges that
the notion "will require some further clarification." He is in
effect inviting the clarification, which shortly after he provides
at some length. After providing the clarification, he points out
that his use of "represent" and "representation" could be completely eliminated in favor of the technical explanations he provided in the clarification. Yet it is convenient not to replace
them because those vague terms are shorthand for complex
syntactic constructions. Notice, then, how vague language can
be rhetorically effective: it gives a reader an intelligible entrance
to an essay; it moves the essay forward by inviting further
clarification and encouraging brevity.

Indeterminateness is still different from ambiguity and
vagueness. Indeterminateness is a kind of incompleteness. It
is symptomatic of the lazy and half-formed thought. Consider
the sentence "Humans are selfish." This sentence is indeterminate, because it does not specify whether all or only some
humans are being referred to, nor whether they are always
or only sometimes so. There are important differences in the
truth-conditions of these propositions:

All humans are always selfish.
All humans are sometimes selfish.
Some humans are always selfish.
Some humans are sometimes selfish.

There are all sorts of ways in which a proposition might be
indeterminate, and it is impossible to enumerate them here.

So one must always be on guard against indeterminateness. Indeterminateness is also one reason why the passive voice is often offensive. Some philosophers assert, "The world is constituted," as if this expressed a complete thought. But what we want to know is who or what constitutes it, not to mention what "constitute" means in this case. The sentence "The world is constituted" would be less misleadingly written, "The world is constituted by_____." This sentence schema would at least make clear that something is missing. It is not sufficient to complete the sentence in this way: "The world is constituted by consciousness," because even this sentence does not make specific what consciousness is involved. There are at least three obvious possibilities:

The world is constituted by God.
The world is constituted by each human consciousness.
The world is constituted by human consciousness collectively.

Which way is the original statement to be taken?

It is tempting to write indeterminate sentences. They are often pithy, intriguing, and epigrammatic. They give the appearance of depth, yet they are shallow. They lack the depth that comes from hard thinking. And they unjustifiably spare the author the effort of thinking an issue through completely. Don't spare the effort.

After writing a draft of your paper, it is a good thing to go over your draft and look up key terms in either a dictionary or thesaurus to see whether there isn't a more precise word for what you mean. Often the more precise word is a bigger word or an unusual one. If that is so, then use it. But do not use the bigger word simply because it has more syllables. (More precise words are often longer than related words because it is part of the economy of language to use the shortest words for the most common purposes, and the precision required for philosophy is uncommon. Philosophers often need to use unusual words because their thoughts are unusual.)

3   Conciseness

Conciseness combines brevity and content. Being concise means conveying a lot of information in a brief space. Brevity, perhaps, does not call for much comment. It is desirable because it typically makes fewer demands on the reader's attention and understanding. An author should realize that she is costing her audience the time it takes to read her writing. A student's professor is a captive audience; don't also torture him.

Although brevity is a good policy, it admits of exceptions. Sometimes the rhythm of language recommends a wordier sentence. Also, sometimes brevity approaches turgidity. That is, it is sometimes necessary to use more, rather than fewer, words in order to stretch out the content of a sentence and thereby make it more intelligible to your reader. Short sentences, dense in content, are often less intelligible to a specific audience than longer sentences with the same content.

Further, brevity does not guarantee efficiency; it concerns only *how* something is said and not at all what is said. In determining the efficiency or economy of a sentence or essay, one must consider content in addition to brevity. A brief but vacuous sentence does not communicate more efficiently than a prolix but informative one. Thus, it is not in itself desirable to sacrifice content for the sake of brevity, although this might be desirable for some other reason: to vary sentence length or to prepare the reader for some complicated explanation. Thus, brevity and content must be balanced. That is the force of the admonition to be concise.

While a short sentence sometimes conveys more than a long sentence, sometimes a long sentence is indispensable. Most concise sentences can be viewed as expressing what many short sentences might have conveyed. For example, the sentence

Descartes has radical doubts about the ability of humans to know anything can be viewed as conveying the same information as these three:

Descartes has doubts.
The doubts are radical.
The doubts are about the ability of humans to know anything.

A large part of conciseness consists of just this kind of economy of expression. But there is more to it than that. Sentence-combining allows the author to express her thoughts in an organized way. The syntactic structure of the concise sentence about Descartes's doubts make clear that the basic idea is that *Descartes has doubts*. The other two ideas expressed in the sentence are subordinate. The idea that *the doubts are radical* modifies the first, and the idea that *the doubts are about the ability of humans to know anything* is a specification of Descartes's doubt.

There are all sorts of devices of organizing and subordinating in natural languages. We have already seen that adjectival and clausal modification can be used for this purpose. Sentence connectives are another such device. Think about the difference between

Descartes begins by doubting the existence of everything, and he concludes that he exists.

Descartes begins by doubting the existence of everything but he concludes that he exists.

Although Descartes begins by doubting the existence of everything, he concludes that he exists.

In the first sentence, the word "and" expresses that the ideas expressed in each clause receive equal emphasis. In the second sentence, the ideas are contrasted and there is more emphasis on the second than on the first in virtue of the meaning of "but." In the third sentence, the idea expressed in the first clause is conceded by the author and the idea expressed in the second clause is emphasized in virtue of the meaning of "although.'

The nuances expressed by "and," "but," and "although," and many other sentence connectives, e.g. "because," are important. Abuses of them are obvious. For example, contrast this passage:

> Although Proclus is the second greatest Neoplatonist, Plotinus is the greatest. Proclus was born about AD 410, but he died in 485. Plotinus's philosophy was organized by Proclus into a series of triadic emanations.

with this one:

> Although Plotinus is the greatest Neoplatonist, Proclus is the second greatest. He was born about AD 410 and died in 485. He organized Plotinus's philosophy into a series of triadic emanations.

You should be able to figure out why the second passage is stylistically superior to the first. Although I can't explain all the different sorts of sentence-combining techniques, you should pay attention to the syntactic structures of your sentences to make sure that they are emphasizing what you want to emphasize and subordinating what you want to subordinate. You should experiment with different clausal arrangements to see which one best conveys your thought.

One way to enhance conciseness is to rephrase some prepositional phrases as gerund phrases. For example, rephrase

> The recognition of the existence of universals solves many problems

as

> Recognizing that universals exist solves many problems.

And rephrase,

The restatement of the argument of Descartes . . .

as

Restating Descartes's argument . . .

Exercise

1   Combine the following sets of sentences into one sentence that expresses the same thought. You may add connectives, delete words, and change the syntactic structure as you please.

(a)   Utilitarianism is a theory.
The theory concerns ethics.
The theory has a principle.
The principle is that one should act to ensure the greatest good for the greatest number.
J. S. Mill is the author of the principle.

(b)   Plato is an author.
Plato wrote the *Phaedo*.
The *Phaedo* concerns the soul.
Plato argues that the soul is immortal.

(c)   Sartre is an existentialist.
Camus is an existentialist.
Marcel is an existentialist.
Marcel is a Christian.

4   Rigor

Philosophers often espouse rigor, which they often explain to be clarity (in some narrow sense), precision, and explicitness. Clarity, especially as it relates to precision, has already been discussed. What about explicitness?

Logicians are perhaps the greatest proponents of explicitness. Yet even logicians retreat from the ideal when they introduce various abbreviations, e.g. the iota operator, and conventions for dispensing with symbols, such as omitting final parentheses from formulas of logic.

Communication in natural languages, much more than in artificial ones, gets along quite well with much less than total explicitness. Total explicitness is inadvisable for a number of reasons. First, it would take up an unreasonable amount of physical space. Second, totally explicit language is more difficult to process mentally than much inexplicit language. (Human comprehension is better when the human has to make some inferences about the material than when everything is explicit.) Third, the author may not be able to say explicitly what he means. One skill needed for effective writing is knowing what should and what should not be explicit. There are then two parts to what a speaker or writer communicates: what he expresses and what he implies. What he expresses is what is explicit in the words he uses. What he implies is what he communicated in virtue of various features of the context of his utterance. For example, consider this essay fragment:

> Immanuel Kant is the author of several, long, classic works in philosophy, including his *Critique of Pure Reason* and *Critique of Practical Reason*. His distinction between noumena and phenomena and his views about the contribution that the mind makes to structuring reality have had a great influence on many distinguished philosophers for the last one hundred and fifty years.

Although the author does *not say* that Kant is a good philosopher, he surely *implies* this in the essay fragment. He also does not say that many philosophers have read Kant's work; but again this is implied by the context. It is highly unlikely that what the author says of Kant could be true unless many philosophers had read Kant.

Although our ability to imply much of what we mean is a virtue of natural language communication, it does cause problems. For it is often difficult for an author to know what he can assume his audience believes and also difficult to know when he has said enough to allow the audience to draw the correct implications from what has been said. In ordinary contexts, people rarely have any trouble deciding this issue. It's different with philosophy. Philosophy is so general that often what one philosopher takes for granted another philosopher finds absurd. Compare the beliefs of idealists with those of realists, for example, or materialists with dualists. The student has another problem. How can a student know what to make explicit and what to leave implicit when her audience, the professor, probably already knows everything true that the student has to say? (For the answer to this question, see Chapter 1, section 1, "The Professor As Audience.")

Being too explicit can result in clumsy writing. Consider this passage from G. E. Moore, who has just finished discussing the differences between such assertions as "I am standing up," "I have clothes on," and "I am speaking in a fairly loud voice":

> But in spite of these, and other, differences between those seven or eight different assertions, there are several important respects in which they are all alike.
>
> (1) In the first place: All of those seven or eight different assertions, which I made at the beginning of this lecture, were alike in this respect, namely, that every one of them was an assertion, which, though it wasn't in fact false, yet *might have been false*. For instance, consider the time at which I asserted that I was standing up. It is certainly true that at that very time I *might* have been sitting down, though in fact, I wasn't; and if I *had* been sitting down at that time, then my assertion that I was standing up would have been false. Since, therefore, I might have been sitting down at that time, it follows that my assertion that I was standing up was an assertion which *might have been false*, though it wasn't. And the same is obviously true of all the other assertions I made. At the time when I said I was in a room, I might

have been in the open air; at the time when I said I had clothes on, I might have been naked; and so on, in all the other cases. (From G. E. Moore, "Certainty," *Philosophical Papers*, New York: Collier Books, 1966, pp. 225–6)

In short, what should be explicit is what is most important. What should be implied is what can reasonably be assumed either as background information shared by both author and reader or as obviously following from what is explicit in the text.

Exercises

1   The passage above from G. E. Moore contains over 200 words. Rewrite it more concisely. Use no more than 150 words.

2   Make the following sentences more concise:

(a) "The first point is a point which embraces many other points" (from G. E. Moore, "A Defence of Common Sense," in *Philosophical Papers*, New York: 1959, p. 32).

(b) By using the recognition of the fact that Descartes in no way refutes the philosophical view of skepticism, we can get a better handle on the proper conditions underlying the concept of knowledge.

8

Problems with Introductions

Well begun is half-done.

Often the hardest part of writing an essay is writing its introduction. When students try to write the introduction first, they often find themselves unable to write at all. Enter writer's block.

One way to prevent writer's block is to write the introduction last. Recall that earlier, when writer's block was not an issue at all, I said that often the beginning of an essay should be written last, not first. However, at some time you will have to face the preface.

In earlier chapters, I discussed some correct ways to begin an essay. In this chapter, I will discuss three ways *not* to begin one. In section 1, I will discuss how authors sometimes slip away from their topics. In section 2, I will discuss how authors sometimes mask the significance of their argument by introducing it as providing the solution to a relatively minor problem. In section 3, I will discuss how authors sometimes begin their essays with a running start instead of starting right in.

1 Slip Sliding Away

One of the most important articles on the philosophy of language is Keith Donnellan's "Reference and Definite Descriptions." Although this article has been influential and exhibits the substantial philosophical ability of its author, it is, I think, a mix of good and bad philosophical writing. Here is the first paragraph of that article in full.

Reference and Definite Descriptions

Definite descriptions, I shall argue, have two possible functions. They are used to refer to what a speaker wishes to talk about, but they are also used quite differently. Moreover, a definite description occurring in one and the same sentence may, on different occasions of its use, function in either way. The failure to deal with this duality of function obscures the genuine referring use of definite descriptions. The best known theories of definite descriptions, those of Russell and Strawson, I shall suggest, are both guilty of this. Before discussing this distinction in use, I will mention some features of these theories to which it is especially relevant. (Keith Donnellan, "Reference and Definite Descriptions," in *The Philosophy of Language* 3rd edn, ed. A. P. Martinich, New York: Oxford University Press, 1996, p. 231)

Consider the first sentence:

Definite descriptions, I shall argue, have two possible functions.

This is an excellent way to begin. It states simply and clearly what the author is going to do in his article. The author says that definite descriptions have "two possible functions" but does not say what those functions are; he neither names them nor describes them. This vagueness is not a defect. It is a virtue. In beginning to write an article it is necessary to orient the reader and introduce him to the topic. An overly specific introduction would not succeed in orienting the reader but in confusing or daunting him. Like an aggressive glad hander, an overly specific or overly complicated introduction would be off-putting. Indeed, the vagueness of Donnellan's first sentence is, in a way, inviting. Upon hearing that definite descriptions have two possible functions, we want to know what they are. We are motivated to read on in order to find out the names of those two functions and what they do.

Donnellan's next sentence is equally good:

> They are used to refer to what a speaker wishes to talk about, but they are also used quite differently.

The phrase, "used to refer," alludes to "the referential use of definite descriptions." This is a familiar philosophical topic, one that Donnellan has every right to expect his audience of professional philosophers to understand. By mentioning the referential use of definite descriptions, he is further putting the reader at ease with the article. The reader is becoming oriented to the article because he is being led into the familiar topic of referring. The second sentence, however, does not lull the reader into complacency. While the content of the first clause of the second sentence is familiar, the content of the second clause is not. It is rather mysterious: "they are also used quite differently." How are they used differently? What is the name of this different use? Is it, like referring, a philosophically familiar topic, or is it unfamiliar? These are natural questions for the reader to ask; they are questions that continue to move the reader forward. The reader has a right to have these questions answered immediately. Unfortunately, this right is violated. Although Donnellan eventually gets around to answering these questions, it comes much later in the article. Instead of either naming or describing the second of the "two possible functions" of definite descriptions, Donnellan changes the direction and focus of the article. He says something that is true of both uses of definite descriptions:

> Moreover, a definite description occurring in one and the same sentence may, on different occasions of its use, function in either way.

While this sentence provides some additional information about both uses, namely, that both may occur in the same sentence, the information does not help to advance the article at this stage. Donnellan has claimed that there are two uses of definite descriptions. He has identified one of them for us, i.e. the referential use, but not the other. Now he says something that applies to both of them. Since we don't know anything about the alleged second use other than that it is not identical with the first, it is not informative to read that a definite description might function in either way in one and the same sentence. We still have no idea about what the second function of definite descriptions is.

The third sentence could be justified if Donnellan returned to the main focus of his article and answered the two questions he raised in the reader's mind earlier: what is the name of the second use? How does it function differently from the referential use? Unfortunately, the next sentence does not answer either question but slides further away from both of them:

> The failure to deal with this duality of function obscures the genuine referring use of definite descriptions.

This is an assertion on Donnellan's part. Presumably, he will substantiate this assertion somewhere later in his article. But the reader has no indication of where; no indication of how; and no indication of how important it is to the article to substantiate that this failure to deal with the duality of functions obscures the genuine referring use of definite descriptions. However, the way this sentence is cast – "obscures the genuine referring use" – suggests that his main interest concerns reference and not the unnamed, undescribed, and increasingly mysterious, second possible function of descriptions. (I do not believe a reader in 1967, when Donnellan's article appeared, could have known this, but the author was indeed primarily interested in the function of referring and not in the other.)

My ideal reader should have the sense that this article is starting to slip away, that his most central concerns are being ignored, and that he has to continue to play the game of reading and comprehending this article without really knowing what he is committing himself to if he accepts that there are two possible functions of definite descriptions. That is, Donnellan is now talking about "this duality of functions" as if the reader knew what both of them are, even though he has not given the audience any reason for thinking that the second function exists, other than for Donnellan's word that it does.

The mystery of the second use continues with the next sentence:

> The best known theories of definite descriptions, those of Russell and Strawson, I shall suggest, are both guilty of this.

Both Russell and Strawson were famous in large part for their work on referring. In his article, "On Referring," Strawson criticized Russell's views as presented in the article "On Denoting." The principal difference between the words "denoting" and "referring" is historical. In 1905, when Russell wrote, "denoting" was the current philosophical term for what Strawson called "referring" in 1950. Again the author continues to discuss referring without any mention or knowledge of "the other use" of definite descriptions. The second use of definite descriptions hovers over the discussion like a specter. (One final point about this sentence is that its last word, "this," is too far away from its antecedent, which is the first phrase of the preceding sentence.)

The contrast between the two possible functions of definite descriptions completely disappears in the next and final sentence of the paragraph:

> Before discussing this distinction in use, I will mention some features of these theories to which it is especially relevant.

The focus of the article at this stage is now firmly on the theories of Russell and Strawson. The distinction between two possible functions of definite descriptions is now firmly in the background. The phrase, "Before discussing this distinction in use" is a promissory note to bring the discussion back to the purported central topic of the article at some unspecified later point. (This turns out to be the beginning of the third section of the article.) There is one further item to glean from this last sentence of the paragraph. Donnellan's use of the phrase "this distinction in use" instead of "distinction in function," suggests that he is using "function," and "use" synonymously.

I have said that the article begins to go wrong after the second sentence of the first paragraph. At that point, Donnellan begins to slide away from his main topic of the distinction between two possible uses of definite descriptions and slides towards a discussion of the views of Russell and Strawson.

There are probably two reasons why Donnellan slides into the discussion of Russell and Strawson. First, the views of Russell and Strawson on referring are two of the most important ones; no discussion of referring can very well ignore their work. Second, Donnellan was arguing for a view of referring that was completely new. He claimed to see two uses of definite descriptions where previously philosophers had seen only one. He was perhaps concerned that beginning with the stark assertion that there were two uses would be unsympathetically received or that the reader would immediately demand to know how his views tied into Russell's and Strawson's. For this reason also, he may have rushed to discuss Russell and Strawson.

Since I have criticized Donnellan's opening paragraph rather severely, it is legitimate to demand that I suggest an alternative:

> Definite descriptions, I shall argue, have two possible functions. They are used to refer to what a speaker wishes to talk about, but they are used quite differently. *They are used to express a unique property that an object has.* I shall call these two uses the referential and the attributive uses, respectively. Neither one of these uses is more familiar than the other. Rather, the two uses have been conflated under the single idea of denoting or referring. Both the

theories of Russell and Strawson involve this conflation and I hope to show that each of their theories describes different aspects of the two uses; this helps account for the apparently extreme disagreements between them. I should say that in fact they are often speaking past each other, one about the referential use, the other about the attributive use.

The italicized sentence above is intended to repair what I have argued is an egregious omission in Donnellan's original paragraph. It is supposed to capture what he means by the attributive use, which he gets around to explaining in the third section of his article.

Let's look at the first paragraph of that section. Here he recovers from the slide begun in the first paragraph of the article:

> I will call the two uses of definite descriptions I have in mind the attributive use and the referential use. A speaker who uses a definite description attributively in an assertion states something about whoever or whatever is the so-and-so. A speaker who uses a definite description referentially in an assertion, on the other hand, uses the description to enable his audience to pick out whom or what he is talking about and states something about that person or thing.

The first sentence names a distinction that the author wants to establish. The second and third sentences constitute a first shot at characterizing each term of that distinction. That is just how an author should proceed. There are, however, some problems with sentences two and three. Although these problems are primarily philosophical, they do show up as stylistic problems also. One of the philosophical problems is that sentences two and three are overly specific. Donnellan intends those sentences to characterize his distinction. But they are too specific to count as an adequate characterization. Since definite descriptions can occur in sentences used to express virtually any kind of speech act: promises, statements, oaths, threats, etc., the author cannot legitimately explain their function only in assertions. A second philosophical problem is that both characterizations rely upon the word "about." This is a problem because philosophers have traditionally used the notion of aboutness to distinguish the referential use from other grammatical functions. So the author's characterization of the distinction between the referential and attributive uses of definite descriptions is not adequate at this point.

2   The Tail Wagging the Dog

One of the greatest articles of the 20th century is H. P. Grice's "Logic and Conversation." It is great because of its novel and powerful theory of linguistic communication and not because of its literary structure, which, I think, is defective. His article begins with a description of a relatively narrow problem in the philosophy of logic and two attitudes that philosophers of different ideologies have taken toward it. The article then proceeds to its main work, the construction of a general theory of conversation, which supposedly has within it the resources to solve the problem. What is wrong with this structure from a rhetorical point of view is that such a narrow and abstruse problem is not sufficient to justify the construction of a theory as complicated and wide-ranging as Grice's. This rhetorical problem is a consequence of a substantive philosophical point: a narrow problem cannot justify the construction of an elaborate and general theory. In other words, Grice appears to be using a cannon to kill a fly. Since the introduction of Grice's article is too long to be reproduced here, I have devised an essay fragment that suffers from the same defect:

Logic and Conversation

It is well known in philosophical logic that the logical constants, that is

&, v, ~, ⊃, ↔, ∃

do not appear to correspond in meaning with their stand-ard English translations,

and, or, not, if . . . , then, if and only if, there exists

Philosophers have typically taken one of two attitudes towards this lack of correspondence. The Formalists think that this is one indication of the inexactness of natural language and say, "So much the worse for natural language." The Informalists think that this is one indication of the narrowness of formal languages and say, "So much the worse for artificial languages." Both groups agree in assuming that there actually is a divergence in meaning between the logical constants and their natural language translations. I shall argue that this common assumption is false. I shall do this by developing a theory of linguistic communication that applies to the use of language in general.

Since it is the theory of linguistic communication that ought to be and in fact is the focus of this essay, its development ought to be the focus of the article from the very beginning. The problem in philosophical logic and its solution in terms of the theory of communication could be brought in at the end of the article as evidence of the theory's power.

With these considerations in mind, the following essay fragment would have been a better way to begin the essay:

Logic and Conversation

The goal of this essay is to develop a general theory of linguistic communication. In addition to its inherent interest, such a theory can be used to solve a large num-ber of philosophical problems. One of these is a problem in philosophical logic, which I shall solve after present-ing my theory. This solution is just one of many possible illustrations of the theory's power.

This way of structuring the essay puts the logical problem and its solution at the end. It is ironic that although Grice motivates his article by proposing to solve a problem, he never does get around to explaining how his theory solves it. However, anyone who knows the problem and understands Grice's theory can figure out the solution for himself.

There is nothing wrong with writing an essay on a narrow topic. What is wrong is leading the reader to believe that the narrow topic is the focus of the essay and not some broader one. It looks like the rhetorical tail is wagging the rhetorical dog. When I first read Grice's article, I was dubious. His theory struck me as unacceptably complex because I thought it was designed to solve only one problem in philosophical logic. Once I realized that that solution was a minor consequence of his theory I was awed by its elegance and simplicity.

One reason Grice's article begins badly is that it was excerpted from a much longer work, his William James Lectures at Harvard in 1962. To mention this is partially to explain why the essay is structured as it is and partially to excuse it; but it does not justify it.

3   The Running Start

Consider this essay fragment:

The Principles of Descartes's Philosophy

[1] The history of philosophy is long and difficult. [2] It consists of many periods – ancient Greek and Roman, medieval, Renaissance, and modern – and many schools of thought – realism and idealism, monism and dualism, atomism and materialism. [3] Is it possible to write a general history of philosophy? [4] Is it possible for any one scholar to read and understand all the work of all the historical figures he needs to, in order to write a general history?

[5] The purpose of this essay is modest. [6] It is an attempt to state the general principles of Descartes's philosophy.

This is an example of "the running start." Instead of jumping right into his topic, the author warms up by talking in the most general terms about the history of philosophy. The thesis of the essay is stated clearly and succinctly, but too late, in the second paragraph. The first paragraph is no more relevant to the stated thesis than it is to any essay in the history of philosophy. So it does not really introduce this particular essay. This means that it should be eliminated. The essay does not suffer the least from having the first paragraph pruned. On the contrary, it is strengthened by it.

One teacher of writing has advised that the first two paragraphs of an essay should always be deleted. This advice is hyperbolic. What is true is that you should check the first paragraph or two to see whether all or parts of them can be eliminated.

You should not try too hard to avoid ruminations that eventually prove to be superfluous. Most people need a running start in order to start the process of writing. Feel free to include superfluous material in your drafts if that gets you going. A running start is better than no start at all. But there is no reason why that superfluous material should remain in the final draft. It should be eliminated in the process of revising your essay.

I have explained that the first paragraph of our essay fragment is an instance of the running start, because it no more introduces the topic of that essay than it does any other essay. Some more specific remarks are in order. Sentence [1] is trivial. Who would doubt that the *history* of philosophy is long? Who would doubt that it is difficult? It is unlikely that a trivial first sentence does very much, if anything, to orient a reader. Indeed, the title of the essay is more informative than [1].

Sentence [2] is not trivial, but it is also largely irrelevant. Little of the detail it provides is necessary for understanding the principles of Descartes's philosophy. The partial catalog of epochs and schools of philosophy, none of which will be mentioned again in the essay, is irrelevant to its main topic. The questions in [3] and [4] are red herrings. Even though they are not rhetorical questions, the author has no intention of answering them. One can imagine the stream-of-consciousness that accompanied the writing of sentences [1]–[4]: "Damn, I have to write an essay on the history of philosophy. . . . What the hell do I know about philosophy? . . . what topic can I choose from 2,500 years of heavy-duty thinking? . . . I can't read all the relevant works . . . I haven't read anything except Descartes's *Meditations*. . . . Ahhh! that's it!"

This brings us to [5] and [6], two clear, precise, and fully justified sentences, the two sentences that express the thought that should have begun the essay.

Exercises

1   Rewrite the following passage in such a way that it avoids the pitfalls discussed in this chapter.

Promises, Obligations, and Abilities

One of the great areas of philosophy is ethics. Philosophers have often worried about what is right and what is wrong. One of the central concepts of ethics is obligation, and we should ask what is the relation between obligation and ability. The issue here can be illustrated by considering a paradox of promising.

(1)   Whenever a person makes a promise to do x, he thereby puts himself under an obligation to do x.

(2)   If someone is obligated to do x, then he can do x ("ought" implies "can").

(3)   Some people sometimes make promises they cannot keep.

Each of propositions (1)–(3) is well supported. Proposition (1) is analytic; it is part of the concept of promising that, if one has promised to do something, then one is obliged to do it.

The distinction between analytic and synthetic propositions is most closely associated with the name of Immanuel Kant and he used the distinction to separate the realm of logic from the realm of fact. Humans have no access to unadorned reality, according to Kant; rather all human knowledge is filtered through and conditioned by such concepts as causality, substance, and temporality.

2 The following passage is an example of an essay that begins well. For each sentence, specify what function it serves. Use the section numbers or descriptive titles from "An Outline of the Structure of an Essay" as much as possible. Some sentences of the passage announce things that will be done later in the paper; express these facts in specifying the function of the sentence. For example, if some sentence says that objections will be answered at a certain place, say that the function of the sentence relates to "Objections."

[1] In this paper I offer an interpretation of the argument at the beginning of *Republic* 10 (597c1–d3). [2] The argument – sometimes called the Third Bed Argument (TBA) – shows that the Form of bed is unique. [3] The argument is interesting because it uses the One-Over-Many principle (OM), which justifies positing Forms. [4] But unlike the use of OM in the first Third Man Argument (TMA) of *Parmenides* (131a1–b2), the use of the OM in TBA does not produce an argument which is liable to becoming an infinite regress. [5] Since the TBA is in every other respect a classic statement of the theory of Forms usually associated with the middle dialogues, we can conclude that this theory is not metaphysically bankrupt, as is sometimes claimed. [6] Whatever the problems with the TMA, they do not infect the whole theory of Forms in the middle

dialogues because there is at least one instance of a clear enunciation of the theory which does not fall prey to the infinite regress of the TMA.

[7] In section 1 of this paper, we analyze the TBA and add three assumptions necessary to make it valid. [8] As well, we explain these assumptions and offer textual evidence for them. [9] In section 2, we survey recent commentaries on the TBA and defend our interpretation against these commentaries. [10] In particular we show that, under our interpretation, the TBA is not liable to being turned into an infinite regress of Forms of bed. [11] In section 3, we see what implications this latter fact has for a theory of Forms which holds that the Form of f is, in some way, itself f. [12] We show in what way this central doctrine of the middle dialogues theory of Forms can be held without threat of inconsistency or infinite regress. [13] In section 4, we apply our interpretation of the TBA to the TMA, showing that the fallacious step of the TMA can be brought to light by considering the important differences between the two arguments. (Richard D. Parry, "The Uniqueness Proof for Forms in *Republic* 10," *Journal of the History of Philosophy* 23 (1985), pp. 133–4)

Appendix A:
"It's Sunday Night and I Have an Essay Due Monday Morning"

You have already promised God that if He gets you out of this mess, you will never wait to write your essay until the night before it is due. What do you do now?

The first thing to do is to think about your topic. The topic may have already been assigned or you may be allowed to choose from several, such as:

the nature of universals;
the nature of free will;
the concept of determinism;
the relationship between mind and body;
Plato's theory of the Good;
Anselm's ontological argument;
Descartes's use of *cogito, ergo sum*.

The next thing you should do is to make your topic more specific. The easiest way to do this is to transform your topic into a thesis. Notice that the topics listed above are formulated as noun phrases. They do not commit the author of an essay to any particular position. The topic, the problem of universals, does not require that the author argue either for or against the existence of universals. It is important for you to transform your topic into a sentence that does commit you to some particular position, such as

> There are no universals. (Only particulars exist.)
> No humans have free will.
> Determinism is true.
> Mind and body are identical.

For our purposes, it is not important whether you argue that there are or are not universals. What is important is that you commit yourself to one position or the other. Your thesis, whatever it is, motivates everything that you write in your essay. It is what causes everything else to hang together in an engaging way. To change the metaphor, your thesis gives you a perspective on the problem and helps shape what you will say and how you will say it.

The next thing you need to do is to think of reasons why a rational person should believe the position you have chosen to defend. Your professor is not interested in how you *feel* about the proposition but in how you view the world. He is interested in how well you can *argue* for your position. You should have read about valid, sound, and cogent arguments in Chapter 2 quite some time ago. But it is too late now to read it for the first time. You will have to rely upon your intuitions as to what counts as good reasons or sufficient evidence for believing something. To put it another way, why should any rational person believe your position?

Don't just think about these reasons; write them down. If possible, work these reasons into a brief outline. Ask yourself which reasons are the most important and which ones are less important. Which reasons are subordinate to which others; that is, which reasons support other reasons for your position?

There is now only one more thing that needs to be done before you begin writing; to think about the qualities you want to aim at in your writing. I suggest you choose these four: clarity, precision, orderliness, and simplicity.

Clarity is important because your first obligation is to communicate with your audience. If your professor does not understand what you are getting at, it is very likely that you will get a bad grade.

Precision is important because it makes your essay more informative. Vague, inexact, ambiguous, or otherwise imprecise language is less informative than precise language.

Orderliness contributes to clarity; it makes your argument easier to understand. Your reader ought to know at all times where your argument is taking him; how he is going to get there, and where he is at any particular point.

Finally, simplicity is important. Keep your syntax as simple as possible. This does not mean that your sentences need to be short or choppy. The syntax of your sentence should only be as complicated as the thought you want to express requires. Use subordinate clauses when one thought is genuinely subordinate to another. Students often try to write complicated sentences because they (think that they) were taught to do so in high school. What they should have been taught is how to write complicated sentences when such sentences were necessary but not to write them as a matter of course or to mimic profundity.

Now begin writing. But do not try to write your essay in one draft. Your first draft should be a short version of what you intend the completed essay to look like. That is, in 50 to 150 words, write a draft in which you put only the most important reasons for your thesis.

Once this is done, rewrite your original draft. Expand it by filling in some of the details you need in order to make your original draft more intelligible or persuasive. Your second draft should be somewhere between 50 and 100 percent longer than the first one – precisely how much longer depends upon how long the original is and how much more you can think of at the time.

Continue rewriting and expanding in this way until you are within the word limits that your professor set. (I am not being sarcastic. You have an obligation to work within the limits set by your professor, and word limits are a kind of limit. Professional writers are restricted to word limits all the time.)

This method of successive elaboration, which was discussed in Chapter 4, does not increase the time it takes to write your essay if you are using a computer. You simply insert the additions at the appropriate place, and the word processing program makes the required adjustments.

One advantage of the method of successive elaboration is that you never lose sight of the basic structure of your essay. Whenever you add something you know why that particular place needs further elaboration in order to contribute to the whole. Another advantage is that each part of the essay has the right proportion relative to all the other parts. If one part of the essay begins to overshadow the others, it can be brought back into line by expanding the other portions in successive drafts. However, you might alternatively find that if one part naturally grows while the others remain stunted, then the naturally growing part may be the one that should be nurtured and the others pruned in editing. If you add material to each part of the essay in each draft, then no part should be overdeveloped or underdeveloped.

Appendix B:
Glossary of
Philosophical Terms

This glossary is very selective. It consists of both technical and stylistic terms. If a term is not included in the glossary, check the index for a possible discussion of it in the body of the text.

act/object ambiguity Some words are ambiguous between meaning some activity and meaning the result of that activity, for example, the word "building." Philosophers have been concerned about the ambiguity of such terms as "action" (it may refer to the event or the result of the event); "reference" (it may mean the activity of referring or to the object referred to (the referent)); "statement" (it may refer to the activity of stating or its result). The same phenomenon is sometimes called the distinction between process (act) and product (object).

ad hoc (literally: to this thing) Something invented or devised for one specific thing, typically to save a theory at the brink of refutation, and not independently motivated or justified by some general or theoretical principle.

ad hominem (literally: against the man) (1) It is usually used to designate the fallacy of inferring that what someone said is false because of his personal characteristics (such as physical appearance, religious or political affiliation) or his circumstances (such as his financial condition or his social relationships). However, it is not a fallacy to consider a person's personal characteristics or circumstances as part of the evidence for evaluating whether what he says is true or false, reliable or not. (2) It is sometimes used to refer to the valid argument tactic of showing that your opponent's principles commit him to a position that he does not approve of.

ad infinitum (literally: to infinity)   The phrase is often used in discussions of infinite regress. If everything in motion must be put in motion by something else that is in motion, then this process must go on without any end, that is, *ad infinitum*.

a fortiori (literally: all the more so)   If all humans are very cruel, then *a fortiori* some humans are unpleasant.

a priori/a posteriori (literally: from the prior/from the later) The first term is typically used to refer to what is epistemologically *prior* to or independent of sense experience, such as knowing mathematical truths "(2 + 2 = 4)" or tautologies ("A white horse is white"). The second term is typically used to refer to what epistemologically comes from or as the result of sense experience, such as knowing what colors, smells, and sounds are. These epistemological terms should not be confused with the logical or metaphysical terms necessity/contingency.

argument   A series of propositions that are intended to give an audience reasons for believing something. The propositions expressing the reasons are called "premises;" the proposition expressing what is to be believed is called "the conclusion." In the example below, the first two propositions are premises, the last is the conclusion:

> All humans are mortal.
> Socrates is human.
> ———————————
> Socrates is mortal.

(See also SYLLOGISM.)

assertion A proposition (something that is true or false) expressed by someone without giving any evidence or argument for it. There may or may not be evidence that could be given for an assertion if it were demanded (cf. ARGUMENT).

causa sine qua non (literally: cause without which not) A necessary condition.

ceteris paribus (literally: other things being equal) A gorilla is stronger than a human *ceteris paribus* (for example, both being in equally good or bad health, both being judged by the same criteria of strength).

compatibilism See DETERMINISM.

counterexample An example that goes counter to something; that is, an example that shows some proposition to be false or some argument to be invalid. "A counterexample to the proposition that no nonhuman animals have facial expressions is the fact that chimpanzees do."

de dicto/de re (literally: concerning what is said / concerning the thing) Often used with respect to necessity. All bachelors are necessarily (*de dicto*) unmarried, because of the meaning of the words "bachelor" and "unmarried" and not because of something inherent in the people who are bachelors. Humans are necessarily (*de re*) rational because of their inherent nature and not because of the meaning of the word "human" and "rational." The meaning of the word simply reflects the fact about the thing itself. The distinction is also applied to cognitive states such as belief. If Adam believes that murderers are criminals, then his belief is probably *de dicto*: Adam believes the sentence "Murderers are criminals." If Adam believes that Beth is a murderer (because he saw her do the crime), then Adam's belief is *de re*: Adam has a belief about Beth and what he believes is that she is a murderer.

de facto/de jure (literally: concerning a fact / concerning what is right)   If an unjust rebellion succeeds, then the rebel leader is the *de facto* ruler though he may not be the *de jure* one.

determinism   The doctrine that every event has a cause. Determinism is often understood to exclude the possibility of free will, when free will is understood as a faculty or ability to choose or act in ways that are not determined or constrained by prior causal events. However, according to the doctrine of Compatibilism, free will and determinism are compatible or mutually possible. Being free, according to some versions of compatibilism, means that the causes of one's choices are one's desires.

eo ipso (literally: by this very thing).

epistemology/metaphysics   Epistemology is the study of what can be known and how it is possible. Metaphysics is the study of the most general features of reality.

equivalent   Propositions are materially equivalent if they have the same truth-value: "Snow is white" and "Grass is green" are materially equivalent. Propositions are logically equivalent if they have the same truth-value in every possible situation, for example, "Beth is rich and happy" and "It is not the case that Beth is either not rich or not happy."

equivocation   To equivocate is to use a word with one meaning in one place and with a different meaning in another place, as if it had the same meaning in both places, for example, "Since Mary was determined to go to the party, and every action that is determined is not freely chosen, Mary did not freely choose to go to the party." The word "determined" in the first occurrence means "firmly resolved" but "was caused by nonvoluntary causes" in the second.

ex nihilo (literally: out of nothing)   God supposedly made the world *ex nihilo*.

false dichotomy   Used in two senses: (1) It applies to a dichotomy that does not exhaust the alternatives and hence is not true, for example, "The US must either use nuclear weapons against Haiti or not go to war at all." A third alternative, not mentioned in the example, is using conventional weapons against Haiti. (2) It applies to a choice that is forced between two alternatives that are compatible with each other: "You must either go to the football game or be with your child." Both are possible if one can take the child to the game.

fine-grained   Usually used comparatively about distinctions. The distinction between humans and nonhumans is not as fine-grained as one that distinguishes among races.

flesh out   To explain in greater detail: "Jones needs to flesh out the skeleton of his argument." (Often mistakenly thought to be "flush out.")

free will   See DETERMINISM.

in se   See PER SE.

intuition   (1) The judgment a person makes before he thinks about the issue seriously; it is the commonsense view. The adverbial form is often used ("Intuitively, human beings have free will and are not constrained by earlier causal chains"). Intuitions can either be proven wrong by presenting theoretically well-established principles that conflict with them, or they can be supported by theoretically well-established principles. Intuitions are starting points for philosophical reflection.

(2) A nonsensible, nondiscursive faculty or method of knowing the truth about profound or difficult issues. Neoplatonist and idealist philosophers often appeal to intuition and appeal to its great value.

(3) In Kant's philosophy, nonconceptualized, perceptual experience.

intuition pump   Any example that effectively illustrates or strengthens an INTUITION (in sense (1) above).

ipse dixit (literally: he himself has said it)   This means that the pronouncement is authoritative. The phrase is often used disparagingly against a person who does not argue for his position, because in philosophy a position needs to be grounded in reasons or argument, not in the authority of a person.

limiting case   If you think of things that belong to a certain type as spread out on a spectrum from most to least, then the things at each extreme are the limiting cases. If Socrates is the wisest of humans and Simple Simon is the most foolish, then Socrates and Simon are limiting cases of wisdom.

materialism   The doctrine that only material objects and their relations exist. It denies that mental objects exist or are anything other than material objects or manifestations of the functioning of material objects.

metaphysics   See EPISTEMOLOGY.

modal fallacy   Because the location of a modal word, such as "possibly," "necessarily," and "must," is important to the sense of a sentence, fallacies are sometimes committed by mistaking what the modal word modifies. It is fallacious to go from "If John was a murderer, then he must have been a killer" and "John was a murderer" to "John must have been (necessarily was) a killer."

mutatis mutandis (literally: changing what needs to be changed)   "It is people, not proper names, that primarily refer to things; the same holds for predicates, *mutatis mutandis*." (That is, it is people, not predicates, that primarily predicate properties.)

necessity/contingency   What is necessary is what must be true, what cannot be other than it is; it is what is true in every possible world. What is contingent is what happens to be true but need not have been; it could have been different; it is true in some but not all possible worlds. See also, DE DICTO/DE RE.

non sequitur (literally: it does not follow)   Any fallacy that involves going from a premise or premises to a conclusion that is not validly derived. The lawyer's fallacy is a *non sequitur*: "Since someone needs to defend the accused person, I need to defend him." This fallacy is usually committed only when a lot of money can be made from taking the case.

obtain   Conditions are said to *obtain* when they are fulfilled or satisfied: "If x has injured y, then one of the preparatory conditions for x's forgiveness of y obtains."

per se/in se (literally: through itself/in itself)   Essentially: "Happiness is good *per se* or *in se*."

possible worlds   Ways in which the world might have been. The actual world is one possible world. Many philosophers think of possible worlds as something like consistent sets of propositions that describe every possibility ("maximal consistent sets of propositions") and that they are useful fictions. In contrast, David Lewis thinks that each possible world is really real for the people in them and that our favoritism towards the (our) actual world is parochial.

prima facie (literally: on first appearance or at first sight)   When this phrase is used, it usually is a signal that the author will show that what appears to be true is in fact not true. The phrases *"prima facie* rights" and *"prima facie* obligations" have been used in two very different senses: (1) things that look like rights but in fact are not; (2) genuine rights that can be superseded by other more important rights.

properties   Often used interchangeably with "qualities," "characteristics," and "universals." Properties are typically anything that is expressed by the predicate of a sentence. For example, redness, tallness, and squareness are properties because "is red," "is tall," and "is square" are predicates. Two exceptions are existence and truth. Many philosophers do not think that "exists" and "is true" express properties.

quantifier shift fallacy Because the order in which quantifier words occur in a sentence is very important, a fallacy often results from interchanging them. It is fallacious from "Everything begins to exist at some time" to infer "At some time everything begins to exist." And it is fallacious from "Everyone loves someone" to infer "Someone loves everyone."

realism Has many senses, e.g. in general metaphysics, a realist believes that the physical world exists independently of human minds. With respect to universals, a realist believes that she exists independently of other minds. In ethics, a realist believes that ethical propositions are made true by some kind of fact (usually nonnatural facts).

realized A mental phenomenon is realized in a brain state when the brain state is the physical basis or foundation for the mental phenomenon. It is possible that the same mental phenomenon could be realized in different physical states.

received view The standard view, the conventional wisdom, or the opinion typically held by experts. The term is often used disparagingly.

reductio ad absurdum A method of argument that begins with the opposite of the proposition that is to be proved. From that opposite, one shows that absurd consequences follow. Since the opposite is absurd, the proposition to be proved must be true.

sine qua non (literally: cause without which not) A necessary condition.

special pleading The fallacy of judging certain members of a group according to one standard and other members of the same group according to a different standard. For example, suppose that Jones is given a job as a scientist because he has a Ph.D. from Harvard but Smith is denied the same kind of job because she is a member of religion X or political party Y.

strong/weak As applied to arguments and ideas, what is stronger has more content and excludes more things than what is weaker. "Strong" and "weak" are value-neutral. Sometimes it is better to use a weaker sense of some word, to use a weaker argument, or to espouse a weaker proposition than to use a stronger one. It depends on the context. ("There are two senses of punishment. In the weaker sense, punishment is any suffering inflicted by an authority for a real or imagined crime. In the stronger sense, punishment is only that suffering inflicted by an authority for a crime actually committed by the person who suffers.")

sui generis (literally: of its own kind)   The phrase means that something is unique. It is the only object that belongs in some category.

summum bonum (literally: the highest good)   Traditionally either God or happiness has been considered the highest good by philosophers. Recently, tenure.

syllogism Any argument that has exactly two premises.

tabula rasa (literally: a clean slate)   Empiricists think that the mind is a *tabula rasa* when a human is born. All ideas come from sensation and in effect write on that slate of the mind.

thought experiment A made up or imagined situation that is supposed to show something, usually something about the limits of a concept. For example, a famous thought experiment that is designed to show that computers do not genuinely understand begins, "Suppose that a person is inside a room into which pieces of paper covered with Chinese writing are given to him. His job is to look up those characters and then . . ."

tu quoque (literally: you too)   The name of a fallacy, which responds to a charge of wrongdoing by arguing that the objector has done the very same thing. It is a fallacy because if the wrongdoing of Jones is the focus, then the wrongdoing of Smith is irrelevant. Roughly, two wrongs do not make a right.

universal/particular   These are contrasting terms, which must be understood together. A universal is what is general or common to many particular things. A particular is what has or instantiates a universal. Fido, Bowser, and Spuds are particular things that instantiate the universal *dog*. Caesar, Elizabeth I, and Napoleon are things that instantiate the universal *human being*. Roughly, subjects express or refer to particulars and predicates express or refer to universals. E.g. in the sentence, "Fido is a dog," Fido is one particular dog but being a dog is common to many things.

unpack (an argument or idea)   To analyze or explain.

weight   A value assigned to something taking into account its importance relative to other things. Being the lawgiver of the Hebrews has more weight than being saved from the bulrushes as an infant, when we are concerned with establishing the identity of, say, Moses. *A weighted most* is the thing that scores the highest points taking weights into account. Suppose that Jones can choose one and only one prize: either one house, which she rates at 100 units of satisfaction; or two automobiles, each of which she rates at 30 units of satisfaction; or 8 dresses, each of which she rates at 10 units of satisfaction. Then the house is the weighted most satisfying object (100 units, determined by multiplying 100 by 1). The dresses are the second most desirable (80 units); and the automobiles are the least most (60 units). Or, to return to Moses, think of some descriptions that are believed to apply to Moses:

saved from bulrushes as a child: 1
brother of Aaron: 2
Hebrew prophet: 5
greatest lawgiver of the Hebrew people: 20
lived before 1,000 BC: 10

Some of these descriptions are more and some less important to the identity of Moses, as indicated by the numbers.
Moses is the object described by the weighted most of these
descriptions.

Index